CLARITY QUEST

Discover exactly who YOU are.

CIEL ELLIS

Candice,
Thank you for diving into this work. May it inspire you to find your Clarity and magnificence.
Love
Ciel

THE ELLIS INSTITUTE

CONTENTS

Reviews

Ciel Ellis writes from a deep well of experience that reminds me that anything can be transformed. She shares her story generously along with simple and effective tools that helped her heal and grow beyond life's circumstances. There's no "expert" voice telling you what to do. Instead, Clarity Quest reveals a woman who's done the work and now, leads other women on the path to healing and leadership in their own lives. A must-read for anyone struggling with their past and wanting to create a new future.

- Sandi Amorim

In this book you will find more than concepts; you will find practical exercises that help to understand what blocks you in your life from having or doing what you really want. This is the most powerful book I have read so far on personal growth. If you want to achieve your goals and have the life you want, this book can definitely help.

- Suzanne Vaudrin

A fun-filled, gentle, yet firm approach to learning more about what makes you tick and what dream to achieve. Ciel draws on extensive experiences in facing life head on, learning from it, and harnessing truths into action. She has written a book full of exercises that help the reader to gain clarity, because she knows that one can't go on a quest by just thinking about it. You will enjoy this book!

- Jeff Jacobsen

So many of us search for answers, often outside of ourselves. Yet we often find our power when we take an honest look and let go of what no longer serves us. Ciel has done this in many ways. Clarity Quest provides multiple approaches to finding your creativity and living from the inside out. “What if your character, which was criticized in the past, is your greatest asset?” Ciel gently guides you to help bring out your best.

- Stephanie McAuliffe

Ciel Ellis writes with a voice that knows--that's been there--a person who truly understands what it's like to struggle with life's big issues and work through those struggles to the other side where happiness, contentment, and joy live. Ciel shares her own story and then provides simple roadmaps and guidance for what worked for her--and what's likely to work for you. I loved the simplicity, clarity and fresh "voice" of this book. I've read a lot of "self-help" guides and have used a fair amount myself and can vouch that Ciel's candid and direct methods and suggestions are real and unique and helpful. Not only will I use this work myself, I'll be recommending Clarity Quest for friends and clients. I highly recommend this book!

- Pamela Sampel

Life is all about choices, and this book will help you make choices that work for you and lead to a more fulfilling life. I love the way Ciel makes you see things in a different light.

- Angela Hook

Ciel guides you through your old beliefs and helps you kick these unsupportive limitations to the curb... with love. Her encouragement to believe in yourself and create a life that you love are intertwined with exercises to help you unblock your self-sabotaging habits. An easy read that is best done in a comfy chair, with a blanket, a cup of tea, and lots of blank pages in your best journal. This book will help you get clarity on the real, beautiful you.

- Jeany B.

This could be the personal transformation handbook you have been waiting for Author Ciel Ellis leads you on a powerful journey of self-exploration, sharing a wealth of hands-on tips and personal stories that will help you find the clarity you need to create the success you desire.

- Sandy Dow

Ciel did a great job in writing this book and it's an easy read. She takes you on a deep dive of discovery. I love her vulnerability and she has such a great way of expressing herself. Really helping me to look at myself and my journey. Thanks Ciel. Definitely recommend to my friends and community.

- Audrey Watson

Ciel authentically guides her reader through the process of

accessing their inner potential to gain clarity in their lives. The exercises will prompt you to delve deep into your past and question how you are engaging in your present life in order to bring forth the future you desire. She shares relatable personal experiences from her journey and how those experiences shaped her inner limiting beliefs. Ciel's growth emerged from identifying, acknowledging and choosing to liberate herself to live a more fulfilling life and she encourages you to do the same by following the processes in "Clarity Quest." I found it to be an insightful and easy read and intend to use the journalling exercises when I feel triggered.

- Jennifer Gray

I so enjoy hearing that my struggles are not dis-similar to women everywhere! I am also grateful to have heard your story Ciel! Thanks for sharing, I have been using the techniques, writing suggestions and enjoying being inspired to keep on reaching for greatness! An awesome read that I will keep near my bed to refer to often!

- Joanne Pegusch

Thank you Ciel for writing this very personal book about your life and sharing both your story and the tools that you have used to break through those barriers that we all encounter in our busy lives from time to time. I thought your dedication to all the woman that you've met during your journey was touching and appropriate! Congratulations on success of this very worth while read!!

- Trudy McAuley

Ciel's life and professional experience shine brightly in her book

Clarity Quest. I often find the books that have the most use are the ones where the author has themselves experienced the journey and Ciel is one of these people. I would highly recommend and look forward to reviewing again for myself and sharing with others.

- Stacey Bout

I'm only half way through this book but I'm thoroughly enjoying it! Its easy to read, Ciel has shared some of her personal struggles and solutions which I find very refreshing. She talks about core beliefs and how to decide whether they're working for you today. The exercises she suggests are well thought out and are easy to fit into a hectic life. I look forward to reading the rest of her book.

- Karen McDonald

Ciel Ellis has crafted an entire process of uncovering and transforming your belief system into one that aligns with your True self. She writes in a way that will give you the experience as if you are being accompanied through a process that can normally feel very challenging going at it alone. Ciel is there with you through the entire process. And having had the privilege of knowing Ciel as a both a colleague and friend, she has a powerful and perceptive presence like no one else. This woman is living proof that you too can personally transform your life!

- Kindle Customer

Publisher's note

This book is designed to take an intentional look at 12 areas of human experience with the sole purpose of shining a light on intended and unintended influences with the goal of choosing which areas will remain an influence in the lives of the reader. The suggestions come from the wisdom and life experience of the author and do not claim to be scientifically therapeutic.

Distributed by: The Ellis Institute Press.

Cover and Interior designed by Ciel Ellis
ISBN 978-1-7750484-0-4: E-Book
ISBN 978-1-7750484-1-1: Print book

Printed in Canada

Dedication

To the wise women
who have come before me
and those still rising into their greatness.

Introduction

"To thine own self be true."
William Shakespeare.

This quote embodies what my life journey has been all about. Very early on I realized that I was on my own. Partly due to the circumstances of my youth and partly because living my life by someone else's ideals proved to be problematic. As I matured the overarching feeling that I had was that I was 'off'. I didn't feel myself and the experiences of my life were creating results I had trouble living with. I've spent 25 years journalling, reading, seeking experts, and generally obsessing about what changes were necessary for me to be fully myself.

As a result of the quest to live a life that was true to me, I've become a prolific artist, certified goldsmith and custom book binder. In addition I've earned my BA in Visual arts and expanded my training into the realm of coaching and leadership. I devoured every course and program offered with one of the oldest coach training schools around, The Coaches Training Institute.

You see living true to myself and having the professional integrity of proper training are part of my values system. I would describe my cumulative efforts as a creative approach to living an empowered life and leading from the experiences that I have personally lived.

In reality, sometimes I feel like I have eight arms, like a foreign deity, all embracing different aspects of creativity, deep thinking, and desire, with the arms in constant movement, shuffling importance back and forth. It's been confusing, joyful, rewarding, ... all of it.

What I stumbled on through all this enquiry and training was that there were problematic themes weaving through my life. Certain areas, topics, that I came to terms with. Clarity Quest is my way of sharing what I've personally learned, furthermore, I have witnessed my clients tackling the same areas in their lives. I'm pretty sure these topics are also relevant to you. It is the perfect opportunity for you to start to unravel some of the things that have been plaguing you, I hope it brings you comfort, clarity, and certainty. I hope it is a guide that helps you refine your life in a way that brings you greater joy.

Living an authentic life, one where the important decisions are your own, where you know who you are and what you think equates to living a life where you are free to be you.

"As soon as you trust yourself, you will know how to live."
- Johann Wolfgang von Goethe

Love Ciel

Chapter 1: Journalling as a practice of meeting yourself on the page

Have you ever faced down a blank page and had nothing to say? I sure have. The mind chatter jumps in and you are immediately stuck. Let me help you with some of this.

Science behind the practice.

Since the late 80's scientists have been conducting studies that access the affect of personal writing on a number of different factors. Researchers have known for a long time that stressful experiences can cause long term problems such as depression, illness, etcetera, and they have realized that keeping trauma secret caused further damage.

One of those scientists is James W. Pennebaker who works at the University of Texas at Austin. He stumbled on an affect that he didn't expect while studying the affect an upheaval had on students health. He assigned the task of writing for 4 days in a row for 20 minutes about that upheaval. The results were remarkable. Of these participants 43 percent reported making fewer visits to the doctor after this writing experience. Many participants wrote deeply and personally about their lives claiming that they felt the process had changed her life.

As the studies have continued, it has become clear that writing has a far wider benefit than was ever expected.

In addition to fewer doctors visits scientists are seeing emotional writing is enhancing other things, such as immune system functioning, better lung function in the case of asthmas sufferers, higher white blood cell counts in aids patients, a reduction in blood pressure, and having an affect on mood shortly after writing, and in the long term. Scientists are also citing a change in social connection, performance at school and work, etc.

How do you actually do it?

The act of writing is pretty simple. You put pen to paper and capture your thoughts. Easy, right? Not so easy. One of the first things to show up is self doubt, criticism and mind chatter that goes something like this: "this is stupid. I don't know what to write. How is this going to help." Sound familiar? Okay let me tell you how I do it.

- 1) Go pee
- 2) Grab tissue, two pens, your favourite journal, and a blanket or sweater.
- 3) Have a second loose piece of paper for writing down those 'urgent' distractions. You know, the laundry, plants to water, dishwasher to empty.
- 4) Have a timer ready, your phone will work great.

Next get comfortable. In a big cozy chair, curled on the couch etc.

Now you are ready.

The next concerns that come up are usually about spelling, sentence structure and grammar. None of them are important.

Now decide on a time that you are going to write for. Ideally you can commit to this regularly. Every day may be asking a bit much, how about most days? Say 10 minutes? Design this in a way that you can succeed easily.

10 minutes. The only thing you need to remember is keep your pen moving for the whole time. If you get stumped and really don't know what to say next, say that. "I don't know what to say, I really don't know what to say, boy I wish I knew what to say……." We often worry when we get stumped. I assure you, your next idea is on the way. Keep writing what is coming to mind.

Now design a celebration for yourself. I want you to make a note in your day timer that you succeeded in writing today. Give yourself a sticker, use a coloured pen, enter it with a different font in your electronic calendar. This will be your physical marker that represents your accomplishment. Well done!

What about resistance?

It is going to come up. Guaranteed. You are not going to want to write some days. So what is going to have you stick with your commitment? It can be really great to create a goal, like 30 days of writing and number off 1/30, 2/30 each time you succeed. This will be the positive reinforcement you need to keep going.

I heard the other day that a woman didn't want to journal because her anger comes up each time she does. Anger coming up is perfect. You want to clear this emotion from your system. We think keeping our emotions buried is the way to go. That somehow it is better to just keep it locked down tight. It's not.

I use the analogy of the beach ball. You can hold it under the water, for a time. But as soon as your awareness slips it pops right back up to the surface. Your anger is the very same. You can hold it down, for a time. Until you can't any longer. The bigger problem is that when it pops out it usually comes out at the most inopportune time. When you least expect it and often around people that you care about. We must become better stewards of our emotions

Letting your emotions out, in your journal, is a great way to release the pressure valve and diminish the unexpected expression of your emotions.

If you are worried what might come up in your journalling, there is no need to be. Whatever comes, you are ready for it. Know that if anger comes up, joy is also on it's way. They will not occupy the same space. For obvious reasons, the two cannot co-exist. The more comfortable you become with your anger, the more comfortable you will become with your joy.

Drop the resistance. Drop the reflex to this practice. Allow what is coming to you, to come. You are meeting yourself on the page. How very exciting.

The small, quiet voice.

I want to mention a little bit about your small, quiet voice. It is your god self, your knowing self, your inner goddess, your intuition talking to you. We cannot hear this precious part of ourselves as long as we keep ourselves busy.

As you develop your practice you will get more and more in touch with this voice. It will guide you in the most perfect way, it is your inner cheerleader. It knows you better than anyone else. So when it shows up, honour it, say thank you and listen carefully to what it has to say. It will never lie to you.

Chapter 2: How Can I determine what I understand?

One of the biggest areas of discomfort for me was realizing that I was following a set of rules and obligations that I had not chosen. I adopted and adapted to them because I didn't realize I had an option. Until I did....

Are you believing it without even thinking about it?

From the minute I was born I entered into a belief system that I was unaware of. The beliefs of my family, culture, and history. The morals, habits, ideas and behaviours of the generations that had come before me, were already established. This fact is not a problem in itself. Where it became problematic is when these belief systems did not align with who I knew I was, or who I suspected myself to be. I set out to resolve this problem when I began to figure out which ones fit, for me, and which ones did not.

To give you a bit of a back story, I was given up for adoption 8 days after my birth. Because of that, the family I was with, I assumed were my birth family. However, at a very young age I was informed, by my mischievous brother, that this was actually not the case and if I didn't behave I would be sent 'back'. Wherever back was.

Here is the first dilemma.

As a child of 4 or 5 years old, with this new information, I questioned what it meant about me, it threw me into a place of fear and instability, an identity crisis because I now saw myself as different, I wasn't one of 'them', I didn't belong here. And yet here I was. In my young mind, I tried to come to terms with this new information, I was successful at creating a story that I could live with, until adulthood when I realized this old story needed to be revised. I had grown out of it and it was no longer serving me.

Developing this story about myself I was using the information that I had at hand which did not include all the details. I identified with that story because it was a safe place for me to put my thoughts of instability and uncertainty. My story development served a very valuable purpose, it helped me get through a time in my life when I didn't feel safe or secure.

What naturally happened is that I identified so completely with the story, that any other option or perspective was not even considered. I was rooted in this story and felt I had to remain committed to it rather than drop it and invite something else in. This story helped me define who I was, and I was not going to let it go easily, because who was I without this story?

When we take another look at our old stories, from a new perspective, collecting new details, we can see things more clearly. We are then able to make new decisions.

One of the many gifts that came from this life experience was to develop my life on my terms. This is now one of my greatest gifts. I believe that our pain points need to be converted into a point of power instead. This is clearly what has happened for me.

I have developed an incredible strength to craft my life on my terms. I now empower others, like you, to do the same.

Take a look at your own life.

What are the belief systems or stories that you have created that may not be serving you?
What are those stories?
How do you see them impairing your adult life?
Is there a willingness to create a new story?

I know, from experience, that letting go of the old story was necessary for me to create a more empowering one. I did not lose my identity, in fact, I began to find my true identity, it started to flourish and grow.

I want this for you, because when we are living a life of authenticity we have access to the full capacity of our Magnificence. I believe living into that greatness is our life purpose, whatever our childhood experiences have been.

Can you hear the familiar guideline of how you are to live?

I spoke earlier about the familiar beliefs that I was born into. Can you relate to any of these?

"A fool and his money are easily parted." "Don't be too big for your britches." "A bird in the hand is better than two in the bush." Wow. There are so many of these phrases that people use and rely on to make decisions.

Do you remember any of these from your family? The problem with these 'stock' phrases is that they are often loaded with judgement, should's, and hypothetical problems that are not specific to any particular occasion. They are blanket responses that don't mean anything. I feel they were intended to imbue wisdom, however, for me, anyway, they have always fallen short.

Let's pull one of these apart, "Don't be too big for your britches." Obviously it is not talking about actual britches. Rather it is referring to being boastful, and bragging about your skills and abilities.

By definition:
If someone is too big for their britches, they are conceited and have an exaggerated sense of their own importance.

It is really saying don't think too much about yourself. Don't think you are great. And certainly don't tell anyone what you think of yourself.

This is a phrase that is intended to undermine the greatness that you have been given. We were all born magnificent.

- *What is the problem with knowing what our inherent skills are and using them in the world?*
- *Isn't that why we were given this particular set of qualities? To make use of them?*

There is a very distinct difference between bragging for the sake of putting others down or amplifying your skills in order to share your gifts. The schoolyard conversation of "I'm better than you and here's how" is so juvenile and no longer relevant. When you are telling people about your skills and abilities it is not for the intent of putting any one else down. Rather it is to highlight the brilliant gifts that you can share.

I think it is essential to know ourselves well. It is actually the only job we have. To love ourselves unconditionally and find ways to shine our brilliance out into the world, that is the purpose of our life.

"Knowing with certainty, who we are, is the foundation for us being great."
- Ciel Ellis.

How can we be great in our life if we are always diminishing our gifts and abilities? Stop it. Own the gifts you were given and shed the familiar tales that keep you believing small thoughts about yourself. You were created with this particular set of abilities and desires because they are meant for you. They are yours. Own them. Use them. Share them everywhere you can.

My experience has been that when I am able to reveal my greatness the world responds by saying or encouraging - more of that please. "It feels good, damn good." I believe this is what life is really all about. Allowing ourselves to feel good, to spread more love and to share our feel good feelings.

I encourage you to investigate, any time you are feeling small, what might be guiding or fuelling that perspective.

- *Is it a familiar limitation that has been imposed on you?*
- *Ask yourself if I were magnificent what would I be doing, saying and experiencing?*

Then go do those things. Do what makes you feel good.

When did you first believe it?

Now going back to the stories that we create. What is a belief that you are holding? The easiest way to discover your beliefs is to listen to what your gremlin, dis-empowering messages are telling you.

They could be things like:

- *"you'll never figure this out because you were never good at math";*
- *"I'm not worthy of love, money, friendship,____ (fill in the blank)";*
- *"I'm just a ________ that's nothing to be proud of."*

Yikes I find these hard to even write. They are so toxic. It's okay, together we will get through this bog of negativity.

You may have been carrying this belief for some time now, it feels like a part of you. I guarantee this is something that you have learned, you were not born feeling this about yourself. When you were an infant you did not have these thoughts, so it is clear that you learned them along the way.

- *Can you recall where this belief came from?*
- *A teacher, a sibling, a parent, a classmate or a friend?*
- *Where did this first come into your consciousness?*
- *Can you recall?*

If you can't recall the specific place that you picked this up, then perhaps you can recall times that you believed it.

- When was that?
- What was going on?

- Who else was involved?
- What were the circumstances?

I want you to grab your journal and write this out in as much detail as you can recall. This is important. As you are writing, watch out for details that you now understand may have been contributing to this old story.

Let me give you an example.

I told you earlier that I was adopted. I learned early on that I didn't belong to this family so I held myself separate for most of my life. I felt that I was discarded and unwanted. When I was 27 years old I met my birth family. What my birth mother and grandmother told me is that I was so loved that they refused to bring me into their dysfunctional, alcoholic home. Oh. With this new information I was able to build a new relationship to my adoption.

It has always been beneficial, for me, to go back and re-evaluate past events with fresh eyes and collect new details. This is precisely why I want you to look back at your stories and collect some new information. I assure you there is something new for you to see. Go gently because I know our pasts can be pretty painful. Take a peek into the archives, just a peek. Gather what you need and pop back out. No need to dive deeply into perhaps painful memories. Go gently.

Once you have some new information I want you to write out the same event that you recalled, and this time, I want you to switch the tense of the writing. You likely wrote the first recollection in the first person. Which sounds like: I felt this, I experienced that, etc. Switching the tense of the writing to third person which sounds like this: she / he felt this, she / he experienced that.

Do you see the difference? Be sure, when you switch the tense, to include the new information that you now have.

Here's my example.

First person. I was given up for adoption and for most of my life I felt separate, unwanted, discarded and different.

Third person. Ciel was given up for adoption and she felt separate and different for most of her life. However, once she met her birth family it became clear that they loved her so much they gave her a better chance at a greater life than they could give her.

What actually happens here is that you distance yourself from the original story and move into being an observer of the details, which is a more objectivity viewpoint. You are no longer living the story, you are a witness to the story and the possible effects of that story.

This is a powerful shift, give yourself some time after this exercise to digest, settle, and understand anew this past experience.

How do you feel when you believe it?

For many years I could only tell you, on the surface, how I was feeling. Likely my answer would have been "fine." Which is close to saying "I don't know, but you obviously want an answer, so I'll tell you fine, so you stop asking." I could not access how I was really feeling because I had never developed that deeper relationship with myself. I didn't know how else I could be feeling. My emotions were locked down tight. I now know this was a reflex from the depth of the pain that I had experienced. It was a safety mechanism that made it possible for me to continue, day to day, being a contributing human being. So thank you and knowing myself more intimately has been the greatest gift.

Let me ask you, how in touch are you with your emotions?
Do you know how different things feel in your body?

This question isn't coming from a place of judgement, rather an acceptance of where you are right now in relation to your emotions.

You may not know that you can actually feel the difference between a yes and a no answer. It's true.

Let me show you how.

Take a deep breath. Let yourself relax. Pay attention to your breathing. Think about a question that will yield a definite "yes" answer. Something like: Is my name _______? Ask this question of yourself and notice what happens in your body. What is the sensation that you feel?

Now check how "no" feels. Think of a question that will yield a definite "no" answer. Pay attention to how this answer feels in your body. Can you feel a difference? What were the differences? This is a valuable tool to use when you are confused and not sure which decision to make.

If we were to take this feeling detection a bit further and apply the VAK system to it, we can get even more clarity. What is the VAK? Visual, Auditory, and Kinesthetic aspects. So back to your yes answer. You know how that felt.

Now ask yourself:

- *What does that feeling look like?*
- *What shape is it?*
- *What size?*
- *Is there a sound associated with the feeling?*
- *What is the texture, temperature and movement of the feeling?*

Now do the same VAK process for your 'no' answer.

This same technique can be applied to your belief system. How does it feel to believe this idea? If it turns out that it doesn't feel good, then likely it's a belief that could stand to be changed. The measure that I'm using to make this decision is whether the belief has you feel better or worse. Why? Because I believe that we are meant to feel good. Damn good and as David Whyte says "anything or anyone that does not bring you alive is too small for you."

The other piece is that all these little things that don't resonate with us weigh us down. They are ideas that we try to avoid, while, in reality, they are informing every decision that we make. Humans will do almost anything to avoid feeling pain and discomfort. Ignoring and burying the feeling is usually the first tactic which in the long run does us more harm.

As mentioned earlier James W. Pennebaker, and his team of scientists, found that not talking to others about a trauma placed people at an even higher risk for major and minor illnesses compared to those who did talk or write about their traumas. My conclusions, based on my own experiences, are that writing about things that have caused an upheaval improves my health.

What do you believe?

Have you ever asked yourself what you believe? It is actually a more complex question than you might think. What you believe creates your experience. Your thoughts become your reality. If you believe that good things will come to you, then they will. If you believe that you are unworthy of receiving the things you want then you will not receive them. But in reality, it is not that easy. The tricky part of deciphering what you believe is that your belief may be hidden under other things.

Here's an example.

A member of my bookclub decided not to continue because the format was not to her liking. Today she disclosed that she is actually afraid to go through the bookclub because she may discover something that she does not want to see and certainly doesn't want other people to see. This fear of seeing herself clearly was threatening to keep her from this club and learning. I'm thrilled that she decided to continue, face her fear and learn that on some level we are all afraid to see ourselves clearly.

What I also know to be true is that the pieces of ourselves that we are unwilling to take a look at are the very same things that keep us separate from having what we want.

Discovering what you truly believe is essential to loving who you are, and being fully who you are. It is well worth your time to explore this aspect of yourself.

Here are some questions to get you considering what you believe.

What I believe about money is:
What I believe about love is:
What I believe about relationships is:
What I believe about my career is:
What I believe about the home that I live in is:
What I believe about my family is:
What I believe about myself is:
What I believe about politicians is:
What I believe about people in general:
What I believe about travel is:
What I believe about luxury is:

Is this a belief you want to have.

From your inventory, that you have just completed, take a close look and see if these are beliefs that you actually want to have. Like we have been discovering, several of your beliefs have come from outside sources which you may not want to continue with. While other beliefs may not have come from you, yet you would like to keep them.

One of the most empowering things to realize is that you actually have a choice about your life. More choice than you may have realized. The next question becomes what can we do about the beliefs we no longer want to have?

Well, you create a new one.

Which means consciously choosing the new beliefs each and every opportunity you have. Catching yourself when the old belief shows up again and replacing it with your new belief.

You'll remember my adoption story.

What I came to believe is that I don't count and I don't matter. As an accomplished woman I know this is not true, however, that is the hidden belief that I had. The question I asked myself was "If I did count and I did matter, what would I be saying, doing and experiencing?" That simple question changed everything.

If I did count and I did matter, then:

- 1) I'd be firing the client who is disrespecting my time and not following through with her commitments.
- 2) I would be dressing in beautiful clothes, which make me feel amazing, versus grabbing what's easy.
- 3) I would be washing, styling, and learning how to pin up my beautiful hair.

Just like that. All these things came pouring through. I acted on every single one of them and guess what? I felt amazing. I was honouring that I was valuable by acting valuable and feeling valuable.

Becoming discerning about the choices that we make is essential to creating what we most want. I know how difficult it is to manage the mind chatter that inevitably goes on around making choices. I think a lot of creating a beautiful life comes down to managing this inevitable mind chatter. There is always an editor, a critique of what we think and feel, it is a bit relentless and tiring. The practice of moving away from your busy mind and returning to a heart centred connection is the key.

This is where the 'how does it feel in your body' part come in.

- *Can you describe what your heart feeling like when you feel amazing?*
- *Does it feel warm?*
- *What texture does it feel like?*
- *Is it substantial, radiant?*

Use your own words to describe the feeling in detail. This will be very helpful to understand how it feels. You can use the feeling as a measure of how well a belief fits with your heart. For instance if a belief shows up that you are not sure about, you can check in with your heart and measure the details of the feelings against the feelings that you set up at the beginning. It is like a checks and measures for assessing how something affects you.

Do you have a hidden belief that has not been revealed yet?

I want to go back to your inventory of how you feel about things. Remember the list? How do you feel about money? How do you feel about luxury?, etc. Which one stands out as being a bit more 'sticky'?

On a sheet of paper write the belief at the top of the page. As an example, let us work with 'Luxury.'

What I believe about luxury is:

- *It is only for the rich*
- *It is excessive*
- *I do not have the money for luxury*

Then ask:

What about luxury makes you so uncomfortable? (Keep asking this question until you arrive at an answer that feels like a "thunk!")

- It makes me uncomfortable because growing up we had a rich family down the block and they were so rude and inconsiderate my parents warned us to never have so much money that you forget who you are.

What about luxury makes you so uncomfortable?

- I think you have to be really rich in order to have luxury which also means you had to be inconsiderate to someone along the way to get rich.

What about luxury makes you so uncomfortable?

- I don't ever want to be one of 'them'

What about luxury makes you so uncomfortable?

- I knew my Dad didn't approve of the neighbours so I will never be rich so I always have my Dad's approval.

Thunk!

Do you feel how this answer now landed on something that is grounded in your belief? The belief is that if I have luxury, I must also be inconsiderate and rude, and I'll lose my Dad's approval.

Let me highlight how this questioning works. It is important to keep asking "What about ______ makes you so uncomfortable" because this is the question that will highlight the belief associated with this discomfort.

You may want to do this with someone else because when we do this on our own there is a tendency to stop before we get to the root of the problem. Which in this case is the association between Dad's approval and luxury. When the resistance comes up you are likely a couple answers away from the 'thunk.'

How do you develop your beliefs about new things?

I've talked a fair bit about the beliefs that come from our past. What about new situations that coming up? How is it that you form beliefs around them? This is an important question because if we are not adopting our routine way of thinking about things, how do we evaluate and develop our beliefs? Independent thought is essential.

One of the best ways that I have found to assess new things in my life is to check in with my body. How does it feel to believe one thing or another. This goes directly back to assessing the qualities of the feelings that emanate from my heart or feeling self, versus the analytical or thinking part of my process.

I am way better at recognizing and assessing my feelings, to the point that I can trust what I'm feeling. This hasn't always been the case. I used to get all muddled and unclear about what I was feeling. What I now know is that my feeling self and my thinking self moved so fast that I didn't have a chance to 'clearly' feel what was going on before my mind got involved. You may be in the same situation. The best way I pulled this apart was to slow things down. I chose to deny my mind free access to decipher the situation and instead brought myself back to my body so that I could tune into my feeling self.

One thing about feelings that I have come to understand, is that feelings are actually independent of thoughts.

Feelings are something that happen, rather than something that is decided upon. Did I feel something, then think about it, or did my thought create the feeling?

What I know for sure is that what I feel is real. If I am feeling sadness, anger, joy, then I'm actually feeling it. Allowing myself to feel it versus wishing it away is the greatest gift. Feelings are simply energy in motion, that's all.

Far too often we have been told that our feelings are wrong, inappropriate, "do not exhibit 'those' feelings." Mostly because the people around us are uncomfortable with it. They exert pressure on us not to feel that way, they may even exert force on us to change what we are feeling.

I recently heard that Oprah as a child was whipped. She was not only whipped but she was told "stop that crying" while she was being whipped. Her body was being beaten and abused and she wasn't supposed to cry about it. "That's crazy."

I know I have had similar things said to me. For example, my grandfather told me "turn around, go back to my room and put on a happy face." So my glum, early morning, non-cheery self was not okay. The only acceptable face was a happy face.

Have you had similar messages
in your growing up?

I want to encourage you to honour what you are feeling without attachment. Allow the feelings to flow through and out of you so that you can release the energy.

Circling back to using our feelings to help us determine our beliefs. When an emotion comes up about something, listen to it, it is coming for a particular reason. I will give you an example. I was single for many years after I left my first marriage. I wanted time to heal and learn more about who I was before I ventured back into the dating world. Once I did start to date, it got very confusing because the adrenaline kicked in, attraction started, things got unclear pretty quickly. There was one guy that I really wanted to like and have in my life. Yet my subconscious knew more than I did. I would feel all agitated around him. Nothing major, I'd just have this urge to stretch all the time. I recognized that this was not usual behaviour for me. I didn't pay any attention, and we continued to date. There were many things that were coming up as red flags, I disregarded the flags because I really wanted to have this guy in my life. The need to stretch and the red flags, were my intuition trying to get my attention, I know that now.

> *One morning I woke up with such pain and panic going on I seriously was questioning if I was having a heart attack.*

As a single parent this became even more troublesome, I was on my own with my son. It wasn't a heart attack, but it was unusual and upsetting.

I carried on with my day and didn't give it any more thought. Until the next morning it happened again. At that point I was really scared. I laid in bed and questioned what is this about? What do you want me to know? Plain as if someone were standing in my room speaking to me, I heard "this is not the man for you. You must break it off with him."

Okay. That was pretty clear. I followed that voice. I followed what I was so clearly guided to and I have never had a panic attack since.

The moral of the story is that your body knows before your mind does. Do whatever it takes to grow your sensitivity to the messages that your body is sending you. Those messages will not lead you astray.

If you only had your beliefs what would they be?

How would it be if you sourced your beliefs strictly from your own information? What beliefs would you specifically hold onto? If you were to write a list of 25 things that you strongly believe in, what would they be? Lets do it right now.

Grab a piece of paper and jot down 25 things that you would like to turn into your core beliefs.

Some of mine include:

- *I believe that I am meant to be happy in this lifetime.*
- *I believe that I am worthy of love and acceptance.*
- *I believe that I have gifts to share that will assist others in living a wonderful like.*
- *I believe that my joy is catchy, other people pick up on my joy and feel some of it themselves.*

I also know that when we act as if something has already happened then it is far more likely to actually happen. The subconscious mind cannot tell the difference between a thought and reality. In your beliefs, if you say "I am so happy in my life, my gifts are making a difference to my clients, and my joy is with me all the time" then you are acting as if this is your natural state already.

Have you ever lived with a bland reality? Where everything just feels neutral? I'm pretty sure we all have. The goal is to switch that bland feeling into a positive, optimistic feeling. Something like "my body is a temple." When I believe that my body is a temple I make choices that are in alignment with that belief. "If my body were a temple, what would I be eating right now?" Then I wait, listen and respond to the answer.

The responding accurately part is essential.

One thing I've learned is that my intuition is a very quiet voice.

I must get still and listen for the answers. That is the first tricky part. When I do hear the answer I must follow through because if I do not then that small intuitive voice will be quieter and less frequent.

We all know that friend who says they are going to do things over and over and they never follow through. What happens? You learn not to trust what they have to say and you want to visit them less and less.

Your intuition is the very same.

Respect what your intuition tells you, nurture that relationship and it will never lead you astray.

Growing into our greatness is a task that can be really challenging.

If you are having any trouble, message me ciel@ellisinstitute.com.

We can schedule a call and start to sort this out together.

Chapter 3: How do I break my habitual patterns so I can create something new?

When we are unaware of how we are responding in our lives we are unable to create lasting change. This is a routine way of being, coasting through our lives, reacting to the things that come up, missing the chance to intentionally create what we want.

Do your habits really need to be 'broken'?

'Habits' are the things we do without even considering if we want to. Most of the time habits are framed in the negative. "Oh, I have a bad habit of _____ (smoking, drinking, eating badly, staying up late, etc.) Do your habits really need to be broken? When I feel like I have to 'break' something in myself, it is a bit violent . It implies that I am some sort of bad version of a human, that needs to be punished, you don't need to be punished for anything ever again. You get to choose what habits you would like to have and which you would like to change.

This all comes down to awareness.

Awareness is about the consciousness that you are holding

yourself in: violent or nurturing? You get to be aware of what things support to be your the best and what may need adjustment. There is no right or wrong, good or bad, it is just what is. If you are not happy with something, then decide to change it.

What are the habits that are coming to mind that you are not happy with?

Could it be that you feel something and you turn to food to shift that feeling? Is that a habit that you would like to change? Changing the way we behave with ourselves all comes down to awareness. Let's just say stress eating is something that you would like to change because it is no longer serving you.

What are some other techniques you could use to shift how you are feeling?

- *Go for a walk*
- *Stand outside and notice your surroundings*
- *Call a friend and talk it through.*
- *Have a glass of water*
- *Grab your journal and write about the things that you are feeling*
- *Stretch your body to release this clogged energy.*

These are a few suggestions from my own library of techniques. Now think up a few for yourself? What sorts of things would be alternatives to you grabbing something to eat?

If the habit that you want to change isn't about eating. Maybe it's about staying up late. If you weren't staying up late what would you be choosing? Perhaps a different way to unwind after the days activities. A hot bath, a walk, a cuddle with a pet or a loved one.

I find what often helps me determine what I would like to change is knowing what I would rather have. In the case of stress eating, for me, it is an out of power experience, because I'm reacting to a stress and no longer in choice. I don't like that feeling, I would rather have a greater awareness of why I want to go eat in the first place. This is sometimes easier said than done.

Again it all comes down to awareness, when you feel yourself responding out of reaction, that is your moment to recognize you are no longer in choice.

What makes you think your habits need to change?

When you think about your habits, what or who has you think they need to change. Whose criteria are you using to judge that a change is necessary? I guess the criteria that I am pointing you towards is discerning if this is your own idea, or someone else's. If you are doing something that you alone are unhappy with, what is it that you would rather be doing? You may hear your mental chatter saying things like " I should be……, why am I not more……, It's so nice out why am I …." Do you hear these sorts of things?

I cannot explain why we say these things to ourselves. What I do know is that this type of chatter does nothing to improve our spirits. It drives us right into the pit of not enough-ness, depression, and despair. So what can we do about it?

We can find something more compelling to think about. Is there a passion, curiosity, inquiry or skill that would have you focus elsewhere? This may appear to be a smoke screen or simply a way to avoid the negativity and certainly it can be that. The longer we dwell on all the bad things we are doing, or not doing, the longer we will stay in that state.

> *I believe that we were all meant to shine brightly in our lives.*

Yet we get stopped by this incessant litany of chatter. Our only choice is to eliminate the chatter and focus on something else. The tough question becomes: what is the something else we can focus on?

Here is where the curiosity of who you are comes in. Getting curious about what you really desire is important. Do you even know what you are curious about? It's okay if you don't know because we are going to dive in and start exploring that very question.

When the chatter comes up, is it the same flavour all the time? For me it certainly is. I know this chatter is habitual behaviour and not true. One question I really like to ask myself is: If this were not true, what would be true? Then I just listen for the answer. What does my mind give me in return when I ask a more empowering question? Then I simply act on the things that come to me. And guess what? I feel way better.

There have been times when I haven't felt very successful. So I ask myself: If I were feeling successful, what would I be doing? The answer that came was: dressing in clothes that I love, eating crisp healthy food, meeting up with good friends. Things like that.

What would you rather have?

When we are busy focusing on our "not enoughness" what are you saying to yourself? I should be exercising, eating better, spending time with friends, etc. With your should's, your subconscious is trying to tell you what to focus on. It wants more exercise. I know you hate exercise. You hate the gym culture. Do you hear all the reasons why exercise is not a fit for you? Get curious. What sort of exercise would work for you?

From my own life, I have been a run leader in the past where I ran 3 times a week with a group. It was great, in the beginning, because it really helped me stay focused on getting out the door 3 times a week. However, soon my body started to become fatigued due to old injuries, so it lost it's fun. The voices were telling me "I'm a quitter, why don't I just push on harder, you don't have the mental strength to be successful with this." Essentially you are weak. Yikes. That certainly is not encouraging me to get out and be more active.

When I got curious, versus believing all these stories, what I recognized is that I want to move my body.

I want to walk on my errands. I want to do stretching in the morning. These things are really working for me. Once we have an idea of what would work, it's necessary to actually try them out. Inspired action is the next step. No negotiating. And guess what? It is working for me. I feel stronger, more agile, more accomplished and happier with myself. Bingo. I have found the magic formula.

The other important piece is I have taken away the 'fuel' for my negative bashing because I now have undeniable proof of where I am taking action.

Now it's your turn

Pick up your journal and number off 1 to 5. List 5 things that you would like to try out for your fitness. (If in fact it's fitness you want to improve. Fill in a different category if you like.) Then beside the 5 things list a couple of ways you could incorporate more of this into your life.

Keep in mind, to begin with, you are experimenting with what works. You can always adjust and tweak what you are committed to, if it's not quite a fit right off the bat.

Is there a habit that you admire in others?

One of the easy ways to determine what you might like to have in your life is by looking to others that you admire. Are there any habits that you see in them that you would like for yourself? Go ask them. Why do they have the habits they have and what is the benefit they are experiencing? I'm sure they have gone through a process of establishing what it is they need and found ways to make that a routine. Ask them. Have them over for tea, or out to lunch and have the conversation around their habits. What did it take for them to be clear about what they want to commit to and how did they get over the hurdle of doubt and negativity. It's a great conversation to have.

Apart from sourcing information from the people you admire, are there any people outside your circle of influence who you admire? What are the habits you see them adopting and using on a regular basis?

Why is it that you admire these people?

Specifically. What can your admiration tell you about yourself? Often when we admiration, envy, or experience jealousy towards another it is a clear sign that those characteristics are something we would like more of for ourselves. Is this a quality that you want because you feel lacking? Or rather a place that you want to grow into? Growth is great whereas coming from lack only reinforces the differences between you and them.

This comparison is rampant in our consciousness because subconsciously we feel 'less than'. I can't explain why we adopt this 'less than' dialogue with ourselves so easily and so incessantly. However, we do.

I want you to be aware of when and how these thoughts come up because it's high time to create a new relationship with these things.

You are magnificent. Nothing you have done, said or experienced has changed that. And likely you have experienced some things that have you believe otherwise. It's okay. Its a human trait. And it's an unnecessary one that needs to stop.

How does it make you feel when you realize you do not like your habits?

What is it like for you to realize that you have created some routines and habits that you are not liking? What is the internal dialogue that goes along with this awareness? Is it okay? Or is it another place for you to criticize yourself?

Feeling not great in our lives because of the habits we have adopted is actually perfect.

It's perfect because realizing what is not working is really the first place to start to explore your ideas of what you would rather have. I want to remind you of the teaching we did early in the series. Do you remember how we checked in with our body to discern a yes or no answer? I guide you to use this same technique about an uncertainty.

To begin with put yourself in a comfortable position. Either lying on the floor, or sitting, feet firmly planted on the floor with a spine straight and your head nicely perched atop your spine. Allow yourself to close your eyes. Take a deep breath and feel where the breath goes in your body. On the next breath allow that breath to travel a little further, deeper into your system. Keep breathing until your breath has spread out to all corners of your body. Next I want you to ask yourself a question that you know you will get a yes answer to. Something like: my name is __________. Ask the question and allow yourself to feel the answer in your body. What does it feel like? Remember that feeling. Now I want you to ask a question that will result in a no answer. Feel in your body what that feels like.

Do you notice a difference?

What specifically are the differences? Next ask yourself the question that you are unsure of. The question could be something like: Is this, _______(fill in the blanks), the right thing for me? Now listen or rather feel what the answer is. Your body knows. If the answer comes back more like the no feeling then it's a no, listen to that. It's important that we listen to the intuitions that we are getting. Moving away from something that feels like a 'no' in our body, is a major step in the right direction.

If you change what will change?

Imagine that you have changed this habit that you have been challenged by. What actually has changed? What is different? How do you feel about the opportunities of your life now?

Has anything really changed, or is it just that your mind has shifted from thinking the same thoughts? Our mindset has a great deal to do with how well we are doing in our lives. If you think about your life and your mindset as a story, a story that you get to write and rewrite every single day, what story would you choose to write? We have the ability to change our minds even about 'big' things, if we choose. Consider the thing that is challenging you right now. What if you could hold it in a brand new way? What would that way be? What if you were to do a complete flip? You are still responsible for your decision, you can be different with the very same problem.

Here's an example.

I have had a relationship with money that includes receiving large sums, unexpectedly, 5 different times in my life. This might sound like a wonderful situation, at first. And certainly I am grateful for the financial support. However, each and every time the money has come to me, it's been due to the death of a loved one. Often tragic and unexpected. My relationship with money, as I decided was also associated with pain. The ensuing belief system is that money, is somehow, out to hurt me. I know this may sounds illogical, however, this is what it all boiled down to.

When I realized this compression I set out to disentangling the loss and gift of money in order to appreciate both circumstances independently.

What I have come to realize is that I get quite a lot of enjoyment from earning money. I get quite excited about sharing the work that I do and earning the money from that good work that I'm doing.

In recent months I have also reduced my debt and allowed myself to manage fewer accounts. It feels really good. At one time I had three separate credit cards all with their very own criteria and benefits. All except one have high interest rates attached to them. I have paid down the high interest rate cards and retained the one that has a low interest rate. One card. One payment. One thing to work with it. So much easier.

When you think about your life and the belief that is troubling you, I want you to know that if you create a new relationship with that 'thing', life can become so much simpler.

Choose one thing that is causing you grief right now and see if you can pull it apart a little bit. What is the story that you have created around this circumstance? What is the new story that you could write? Give it some thought and let your imagination lead you. Listen to your body and follow the direction that you are given.

What if you could just make a new decision?

Like I highlighted in the previous section. Sometimes our stories and connection to them can just flip. This is important because often we are committed to holding up some perceive value, purpose, or vision of what we should, could, would, be if only ______ were true. What if we could just make a new decision? "This is not working, so I'm going to do something else." It can be this simple. Making a decision does not mean that you are stuck to that decision forever. Change your mind. Be different. Think differently. Recognize the pain, discomfort, anxiety, frustration, the situation is causing you and decide to make a new decision.

I want to introduce the idea here that you need not make a wholesale change in your life to live a very different life. All you need to change is how you are living within this life you have been given. I know this may sound like a paradox. However, changing how you are in your life will give you the firm foundation from which to decide if something major needs to change.

This is really important.

More important than at any other time in history because in our modern world we have all kinds of opportunities that previous generations just did not have. Your mother, or your mother's mother could choose to be the housewife, secretary, teacher, or nurse? Those were the choices. A few strong women made other decisions, however, for the the majority choosing from the limited set of opportunities was all that they had.

Times have changed. We have the resources, knowledge, strength and opportunity to change and create the life we most want to live. And it's still scary and you will be unsure and questioning if this is the correct decision.

Just know that you need not make this difficult. Believe it can be easy and choose something new for yourself.

When you improve your life you make possible new awarenesses, new education, a new relationship with yourself, more confidence, more self trust, more of your voice can be heard. When you engage with your world you bring all of this new confidence with you. You have a positive impact on those you encounter because you are feeling freer and more positive. It's great energy to be bringing.

What's valuable about your habits?

When you think about your habits what could possibly be valuable about them? How are your current habits assisting you? Habits are a very good thing to create structure, routine, and rhythm to your life. As long as they are serving you. If they are serving you, then what are they adding to your life?

For me, I'm a gemini, and fiercely independent. I buck against the structure of routine as I like to be a free living spirit and roll with what comes my way. Not so conducive to routine.

However, when I do commit and create routine I feel much better. I enjoy my life and I accomplishing things with more ease. I feel better about my days.

The tricky part is always watching and paying attention to how the habit is affecting me. Habits evolve over time, they change and morph so if we are not checking in regularly to see if they are still working for us then we are susceptible of getting off track.

It is a good things that our habits evolve because it is a sign that we are evolving also.

Our evolution is the point of all this? To improve how we are living our lives? To mitigate the things that cause us pain and implement more of the things that bring us joy.

The other valuable thing about of our habits is that we get to choose the habits that improve our lives. This may sound a bit simplified, let me explain. Let us say you created a habit around exercise, just an easy practice of doing planks each day. You commit to it and it's going pretty well. You like the results you are seeing and feeling within the first week. In order to expand and evolve this good feeling you could add one additional thing to the process. Say some leg strengthening exercises that you do at the same time as the planks. You are already committed to the one thing, adding one additional thing will grow your feeling of accomplishment without much effort.

What do you wish you never did again?

Here's where the rubber hits the road. The things that you don't like, that you are tolerating, continue to give you grounds to complain about them. From this point on, all complaining stops. Either learn to like the thing that is bothering you or commit to change it.

Angela Lauria, author of The Difference, said that an ongoing complaint is some thing you are actually okay with or you'd change it.

You hate doing the housework.

You have two choices. Change your mind about it and find a way to appreciate it, or hire a housekeeper. You get to choose. What I am pushing you to do is get serious about your life. The things you complain about are taking valuable energy away from your enlivened, wonderful life. I don't know about you, but I suspect we only have one go round at this thing called living, we only have a limited amount of energy, time, and resources. Do you really want to spend it being unhappy and complaining about your life?

The day you were born you were given everything that you need to live a wonderful life.

You are a gift to the world and you have the right to use these gifts. What are you going to do with them? Use your life to be a full expression of your magnificence.

Danielle La Porte broaches the subject of our life purpose and she quotes that all we need to do to discover our life purpose is figure out what floats our boat. Simple, and not simple all at the same time. She goes on to say that your life purpose is whatever you say it is. Who else is the expert in you? No one. No one is living your life for you. It is your responsibility to discover what your gifts are, use those gifts for your good and the good of others and inspire others to express their gifts. Mother Theresa said that if we all swept our front porch the world would be a tidy place. It is an analogy for this principle. If we were living our hearts desire and sharing our gifts, our world would be a much different place. Enlightened, enlivened people or so much fun to be around.

Could your happy with habits inform your not happy habits?

If you were to consider what you know about your happy habits what could they teach you about your unhappy habits? What are you learning about yourself in your happy habits? Are you learning that it is pretty easy to expand a happy habit when you are already committed to it? That you feel great about yourself when you commit to the things that matter to you?

What could these good habits teach you, as a contrast to the unhappy habits? That the unhappy habits are dragging you down, yet you still feel obligated to complete them?

Do not get me started on obligation, oops, too late.

Obligation.

- something by which a person is bound or obliged to do certain things, and which arises out of a sense of duty or results from custom, law, etc.

- the act of binding or obliging oneself by a promise, contract, etc.

We are conditioned to comply with obligation and often meet it while feeling resentment and anger. We: 1)resent the task; 2) we set aside our personal choice for this obligation.

Whenever we respond out of obligation we are responding in a way that is incongruent to our own needs. It is going against what we inherently need. This will always cause us problems as it will deteriorate our own ability to choose.

When we are designing a life that we most want to live, it is very important that we reclaim all these areas that have become pinched or folded in an effort to meet someone else's demands.

Obligation is never good for our soul. Having the courage to make our own decisions is again a valuable element to reclaiming ourselves.

It is not wrong to be selfish, to serve our needs first, particularly when we have neglected our needs for a number of years. It is necessary to swing to a completely self centred view point in order to regain a sense of who we are, before the obligation set in. Just know that it will not always be this way. You will swing back to a more moderate position with more compromise and inclusion, when you have reclaimed your ability to choose. However, you will never regain that sense of yourself unless you carve out the time you need to hear, feel, and experience your own decisions.

In addition, doing things for other people can be a great source of joy when we are choosing to do it and tap into our loving, generous heart at the same time.

Chapter 4: How do I come to terms with my past that won't leave me alone?

Do you feel like your past experiences pop up and run your current life, sometimes? Being susceptible to these recurring memories used to take me out for, sometimes, months. I would be so upset and trying to avoid thinking about it, that I really wasn't present to my current life.

I have bad news you can never change your past.

I know as much as you would like to forget, put to rest, and live separate from your past, it is impossible. It is part of who we are. I know you have heard the saying: "Your past made you who you are." Wa, wa, wa. (Insert the teachers voice from the Peanuts cartoons) Yes, that old saying is true. However, the problem becomes accepting and loving who we are despite what we might have experienced.

How do we come to terms with who we are?

I do not know about you, but my past shows up when I least expect it. It shows up in my quick reflex of anger, my depression that takes me down, my inability to relate to others, my withdrawing because it seems easier, my incessant habit of turning against myself and riding my ass like no ones business.

This is how my past, learned behaviour shows up in my life. Am I proud of it - not always.

The events of my past cannot be changed, and what I learned from those past experiences is pretty established. It is a pattern and rhythm now. Many of the things I do and think are unconscious behaviours that I feel unable to correct sometimes. Maybe that's okay. Some of these things are what makes me, me. Some of these things I don't actually want to change, as uncomfortable as they might be. Can you relate? There are things about myself that from the outside viewer perspective may be negative traits, however, they may be the very thing that gives my voice strength.

One of my early beliefs was that "I don't count and I don't matter."

This summer, we were camping and it always irks me that other campers arrive and put the radio on. When I go to the woods I want silence, peacefulness, calm. Yet, my desire for silence is trumped by their desire for music and I have no choice. The sound travels throughout the whole campground. It annoys me and this summer I had a melt down. I know that the melt down was too large for the actual circumstances, which is my first hint that the reaction is related to something old. My husband, what a sweetheart, invited me to join him around the fire at that precise moment.

I replied "No, I can't join you, I'm too upset."

Off I went into the trailer to journal about what was going on.

I cried and cried and wrote about all the details that were coming to me. It helped so much. This time apart gave me the opportunity to feel what I was feeling and allow it to move off. It was my best medicine.

An outside observer may judge me as being too emotional, childish, over-reacting, etc. Which would be speaking more about their discomfort than anything I was doing. This quality of mine, to feel things deeply may be seen as a negative, when in reality it is one of my greatest gifts. I love that I can access this depth of emotion, allow myself to feel it, and let it move off.

Brené Brown has taught us that we cannot selectively suppress our emotions. So if we are suppressing our anger, our sadness, our discomfort, then we are also suppressing our joy. I want to tap into more joy and the way to do that is allowing my sadness to flow out of me easily.

What if there is nothing to come to terms with?

What if, there really was nothing to come to terms with? What if you are perfect just the way you are, nothing needs to be changed? Nothing! The anger that you think is such a problem, simply isn't. The jealousy that comes up, is normal. The envy that you feel towards others is a marker for what you would like to have more of in your life.

It's quite simple. Accepting what is, neutralizes all these seemingly annoying problems. Have you ever tried to muscle your way though not feeling something? How did that go? Let me guess, not so well. How can we force ourselves not to feel or think something? Well, we can't really. That is the beauty of it. We feel what we feel, we think what we think.

I think what gives us the most pain is wishing something away.

Let's just say you are angry? Why? What caused your anger to flair up? I guarantee you that a boundary has been crossed. Some value of yours has been violated. If, for example, someone tells you that they are going to do something, you expect that they will follow through. When they do not, or they are late, or they miss the deadline, your automatic response may be to get angry.

"You said you were going to _______. And you didn't. You forgot, you didn't keep your word."

Which then has you believe that you can't trust them. All or some of this may be true. There is a lot going on here. What I want you to examine is your anger flaring up. Is your anger a reflection of a boundary that has gotten crossed? Is it about honesty? Being able to count on what others say? Trust? What exactly is it?

Once you pinpoint what is making you angry, then you can more easily understand why you respond the way you do.

By pinpointing what triggers your anger, it is then possible to ask, clearly, for what you need. The next time you ask someone to complete something for you, you can say that you are counting on them to follow through, be on time and keep their word. This gives both of you the opportunity to succeed.

When we speak without clarity we set ourselves up to be disappointed.

When we are clear and people don't follow through, then we get to make a new decision. The decision might be to not rely on that person again or have a different relationship with them. Sometimes people are unwilling, or unable to provide what you are seeking. Compassion for me, compassion for you. If you know a friend is always late, then don't expect them to be on time just because you asked. You are likely to be disappointed.

Empower yourself to have clear boundaries, understand yourself well, and communicate in a way that has everyone be successful. It is so much easier and more rewarding.

What exactly pains you about your past?

Some experiences are difficult to understand and live with. This may be due to the events happening when we didn't have the maturity and cognitive ability to understand them. So what exactly is it about your past that is causing you pain? Usually the pain comes from a belief that was created because of the experience. The belief is actually what is causing us the pain, the event is long over. Taking a look at our past for what the experiences taught us is a window to understand the event and the key to relieving the discomfort.

When I was given up for adoption I believed I was unwanted, discarded, somehow different. One of my adopted brothers also made it clear that if I didn't 'behave' I would be sent back. Wherever back was. What has caused me pain from this experience is that I wasn't wanted in my birth family or my adopted family. "When will I be wanted?"

The belief that I created as a child was based on a limited understanding, it was not the whole truth of the matter. I took what my brother said to mean something about me and turned that into a behaviour of separation in order to honour the belief that I do not belong. It is that belief and resulting behaviour that caused me the pain.

Continuing to believe that I was unwanted is what caused me the pain.

It really is a habit that I created. It is just a habit. It is not the truth. The truth is nothing I've said, done or experienced has changed how magnificent I am. When I realized this, I decided to create a new story of my adoption and adoptive family. I could release myself from the discomfort of the old, limiting belief.

However, in order for this transition to happen I had to have the courage to look at what was paining me.

It was not easy. There were buckets of tears and heaps of anger that went along with this exploration. And it was the only way through. This goes back to the Brené Brown idea that we cannot suppress our emotions selectively. As long as I was holding this old belief about myself, there was no room for the real truth to come forward.

Is there a past belief that is causing you pain? Are you willing to dive in and explore that discomfort? I guarantee you that it will free you and release a joy and self knowing that you cannot create any other way. Today, I want you to explore your willingness and ability to unearth what is paining you. I will reveal how to do that in the next section. If you need help, I'm here to help. You don't have to do this alone. You can contact me at ciel@ellisinstitute.com

Is that event you recall still happening? No? Then the pain is the thought or memory of it.

Ask yourself, is the event still happening? If the answer is 'no' then it is clear that you are feeling bad because of the thought or the memory of the event. This is good news because it means that you can undo the connection with those events. Part of my process to transform my connection to past events evolved into my signature program titled U-Thrive™.

When you think back to the event that you experienced you

may be tempted to latch onto the first thing you recall. I'll caution you against this because the first thing that comes to mind is the routine, patterned way of remembering the event. This patterned way is also loaded with judgement, fear, resentment, misunderstanding, etc. Our ego embellishes these past events so that we can feel better about ourselves. Which also means we likely place blame on others who were involved. None of this is productive thinking. Also, the first recollection of events is likely not the entire story. When we dig down a bit deeper we can unearth some old details that we may have long since forgotten.

> *Let us be honest, this personal recovery work is difficult to do and I would suggest doing it as thoroughly as possible the first time.*

Which means that digging down deeper, doing the deeper work, yields greater rewards in the long run.

So how does the U-thrive system work? The first step is **U**ncovering what the belief is that's paining you, and write it out in as much detail as you can. Then, **T**racing the origin of this belief or event. How has it affected you throughout your life, current and past. The third step is **H**oning in on what you had this event mean about you. What message did you internalize about yourself because of this event. Then, **R**e-write your relationship to this event. This step is particularly powerful because you now have new eyes to look back on these events. Change your relationship to the event and start to live free of the burden you have been carrying. The next step is to **I**magine your life without these events. If you no longer believe these past things, what would you be believing? This is the dreaming stage. What is it that you see possible for yourself? Then the process of **V**erifying which dreams you would really like to realize. If you are anything like me, I have many dreams. However, not all of them are dreams I want to realize right away. We eliminate some them in this stage.

The last step is **E**ngaging with the plan that will move you forward with the dreams that you have chosen.

Here is the website for the institute for more information on this program. www.ellisinstitute.com

How often is your past in your present?

How often do you think about your past in your present life? I think you would be surprised to realize how much we craft our lives around the things that we most want to avoid. Shame, anger, resentment, disappointment. We subconsciously tell ourselves "Well, if I never do that again, I won't feel embarrassed or ashamed." Each time we avoid things, we are limiting our life. Now I'm not saying you should be sadistic and keep creating shameful experiences. What I am saying is, you felt shame, one time, when you did that one thing, with that particular group of people. It will never be like that again. The thing you are avoiding, for fear of feeling shame, will likely never happen again. You can gather some new tools and resources before you venture into a similar experience.

For instance, if you were ridiculed, as I was, during grade 2 math, I've learned that the shame I felt was triggered by that time and space. Since I've undone the shame experience through my process of understanding it thoroughly, I no longer feel shame around math.

I think the most difficult things to be aware of, are the subconscious ways we craft our experiences.

We don't think very deeply about it, we just don't repeat whatever bothered us.

This showed up again for me recently when a friend joined me for my regular walk in the woods with my dogs. While we were walking, her car was broken into, badly. They didn't manage to steal anything valuable, however they damaged every lock, door, hatch back, and glove box. The damage was severe. It took many weeks for her to get her car back.

I hate being broken into. I hate being violated and stolen from. It has happened several times in my life and each time I craft a new way of being in order to prevent that from happening again.

I subconsciously have not returned to the park since. I didn't really think about it until now, however, it is the case that I have not thought to go back.

I loved walking in the woods.

However, the threat of my property being violated at my expense is loathsome. Perhaps there is a different way I could experience the woods. Park somewhere more visible. Put a camera in my car that would record any activity, etc.

I am not a paranoid person however, I have clearly limited my experience based on this event.

Subconsciously there are all kinds of things that we create or don't allow because of a belief system that was created. If it's in our subconscious, you might be wondering how it can become part of our conscious mind? The best way I know is to watch our behaviour and ideas closely for areas that seem suspicious. My not going to the woods any longer, when I used to love it, was a clear sign that something has gotten in the way. My fear of getting my car badly damaged is the idea that keeps me from my practice.

Our thoughts become things.

The more I think my car will be damaged, the more likely it actually will be. Connecting to the joy of the place and the benefit to my dogs and my well being is way more powerful.

I know that with this joyful energy coming to the park with me, I will be less likely to have anything happen to my car.

Our thoughts are powerful. Make sure that you are a steward to what you are thinking. It's important because your thoughts create your experiences.

What happens just before the thoughts of your past showed up?

There is always a moment just before your past comes rushing in. Do you know what those moments are? Are they always the same or do they have a different flavour? If you can notice and collect the things that cause these past stories to come rushing in, you will be better prepared to avoid them in the future. Avoid is maybe a bit too hopeful because we cannot actually control what triggers us. What we can do is recognize what those triggers are, how we respond to them, and see the pattern of them occurring in our lives.

The trouble with this noticing process is that the past comes rushing in, and often takes us out of our awareness before we have a chance to stop it. All this happens in an instant.

In collecting and noticing the things that trigger you, your awareness gets heightened.

Keep in mind this may not happen overnight. It may take some time.

What will soon happen is that you will notice and have the opportunity to make a decision about how you will react to the trigger, you could choose to let it take you out, or you could choose something else.

When I talked about the Pray Rain Journalling, you could choose an empowering thought to replace the reaction to the trigger.

Keep in mind a trigger may be difficult to manage because it often involves our nervous system.

Our bodies react.

The skill that I want you to develop is that of the non reaction. Take the information in, breath, gather yourself, and call up your observer self. This is the part of you that can distance you from the events and 'watch' what has just happened versus being completely immersed in it. This will help you stay in the place of choice, which allows you to decide how you want to respond. Your breath is really important here.

> *When our nervous system responds it directs our blood flow to our extremities so that we are ready to flee, fight or freeze.*

Unfortunately we are unable to think clearly when this happens because our brains are being starved of blood flow. The way to bring this all back into harmony is to breath. Allow your breath to calm your nervous system and bring you back to your place of choice.

Sandy Dow, a colleague of mine wrote a book Thriving in Chaos which addressed some simple techniques to work with a nervous system that has been overstimulated.

What if your triggers were not the truth of who you are?

Very quickly you can be taken back to an earlier event or a memory of something that you experienced. What if that is all it is, a memory? What if it doesn't mean anything? Sure it feels all real and the same emotions come up, but in the present moment those events you remember are not happening. The emotion of it is. We have talked about feeling those emotions, expressing the anger in a safe way, now what?

If that past trigger is not true, then what is true?

Can you imagine the possibility of your life opening up when you are no longer held by the surge of emotion and memory from the past? You have tools now to manage any of those past memories, and it is time to focus your attentions somewhere else. This can be just as scary as reliving some of those memories.

Marianne Williamson talks about our greatest fear being that we are powerful beyond measure. I think that power scares us. We have ideas about what living into our greatness will mean. It could be "I'll lose friends because I will be too popular, people will judge me as boastful, I'll be thinking too much of myself." All these things are possible, people may judge you. I have a news flash, they are judging you any way. We are human, judging others is something most of us can do pretty quickly. However, there is no need to get 'hung up' or distracted by those judgements. When someone judges you it says something about their limitations, world view, and ability to expand into their greatness. They are on their own journey. There is no need to hold your life back because of them.

Back to you. Imagine your life, free of roadblocks, it could be anything you set your mind to.

- *What would you like to do with your life?*
- *What is your unique greatness?*
- *What do you feel pulled to explore?*
- *What are you curious about?*

This gets exciting. The possibilities are so broad.

The opposite may also be true. You may not find this exciting because you aren't able to answer these questions. It's okay. I was there for a long time myself. Simply asking the question means that the answer is on it's way to you. Be open to following your curiosity. You will find the clarity.

I usually jump to build the whole thing, in my mind, without ever taking any action.

In that process my doubt creeps in, my 'committee' arrives to tell me all the reasons this won't work, and why it's not possible, etc. Do you know what I mean by committee? All those voices in our heads that tell us we can't.

Baby steps are necessary here. Start making small actions towards the thing and as you take action, you are creating undeniable proof of what you are capable of. This is a great antidote to the 'committee'. You are then on solid ground with the evidence that you have created movement and experience. The 'committee' can't take that away from you. It is a wonderful momentum building process.

What if your character, which was criticized in the past, is your greatest asset?

What were you criticized for as a kid?

Perhaps you were 'too' shy, too outgoing, too loud, too withdrawn. Any of these sound familiar? What happened when you heard these things about yourself? Let me guess. You tried not to be those things. You didn't want people criticizing you for something you were doing. You wanted to fit in, so badly, that of course you would stop doing whatever was being criticized.

That characteristic may be your greatest asset. How so? People said you were too shy, what is shy? Shy is someone who wants to observe what is going on before acting. Shy is someone who is sensitive and the commotion often becomes too much. Shy is an intuitive who is picking up on all kinds of subtle messages that others are missing. Shy is someone who waits to engage in conversation and may decide not to, at all.

So when you decided to not be shy any longer, to force yourself to be more involved, to jump in and participate before you were ready, you left all these other qualities behind. All the intuitive, sensitive and observation skills had to be set aside in order for you to be 'more' acceptable to others.

This is called socialization and I think it is one of the causes of our disassociation with self.

It became too difficult to keep all of our sensitivities and be social at the same time.

The good news is that there is a trail of bread crumbs back to the place where you set these characteristics down. They are still there for you, the parts of you that were left behind are still a part of you, they have not been uncovered for some time, that's all.

The other important thing to realize is that the characteristics you set down are natural ways of being for you. It comes easily for you to be sensitive. Easy is a great measurement. What if we used easy as a measure of success? What would your life be like if you chose easy?

Authenticity of character is always going to be our solid ground.

If we are being authentic then we are showing the world truly who we are, without the 'set down' parts being left behind. When we are authentic, we are having way more fun in our life, and we are attracting people who like what they see. We will attracts the very people who really enjoy us.

When we are authentic, we are more joy filled. Joy filled people share joy in their circles of community. When we have more joy in the world we have less strife. Being authentic has a ripple affect that you may not even be aware of. Positivity breeds positivity.

It is safe, and it is time for you to reclaim those parts of yourself that were left behind. You can access easy and have your joy spread out around you. You will attract the people to you who really 'get' you, and it will be way more fun. The way to do that is to be authentic. To capture all of who you are and share it with the world.

What if holding onto past beliefs means your future will be more of the same?

Again I have bad news. You have lived your past and it has left it's mark. I'm sorry about that. However, it is now your role to decide if you want those experiences to continue. This may sound a bit harsh and I guess it is. You have to decide what you would like to do with your life. Do you want to keep living the past experiences, or find a way to stop living them.

The best way I know how to stop living them is to:

- *Feel them for what they are.*
- *Highlight what you learned from them.*
- *Recognize how resourceful you are to be here.*
- *Then create and imagine something else.*

I've heard that our brains cannot tell the difference from a real thing happening or an imagined thing. If you can believe, really believe, better things for yourself then those better things are more likely to happen. If you cannot imagine them then they will not happen.

I'll believe it when I see it. Is actually - I'll see it when I believe it.

Does it make you mad that your past keeps coming up? What if you were to take a stand and stop this old, negative belief system? When we change our belief we are no longer victim to those negative thoughts. We have spent a lot of time on our beliefs. What do you believe about…success… money….relationships, etc.

Pick one area that you want to explore.

Success. (Choose a topic here for yourself.)

What do you believe about success? Grab a pen and paper and jot down 10 things that you believe about success.

Here are some examples:

1. *It's hard;*
2. *I'll never achieve the success because I've tried before and failed;*
3. *I always miss something when I'm striving to create something new;*
4. *I feel bad when I don't succeed;*
5. *Success = being aloof and set apart from others;*
6. *Success = Envy;*
7. *I'm not in control of my success because someone else always comes in and sets new restrictions on me;*
8. *My schedule isn't my own so I'm challenged to even get my to do list done each day.*

I think you get the idea. Most of the things I have listed here are simply not true, success can be easy. Your schedule not being your own is definitely a challenge, however, I'm certain there are small moves towards success that you can make which are in your control. What are those things? Where are the incremental changes you could make towards the success you are heading for?

> *With this list I want you to write out the positive versions of them.*

'It's hard' turns into *'success comes with ease'*. *'Never achieving success'* turns into *'each time I've tried I learn new things and get closer to what I want'*. I think you get the idea.

If our brains cannot tell the difference between a real thing or an imaged thing, then start imagining your success. Imagine it all coming together. Feel into the excitement of the possibility and allow it to grow on itself. Success breeds more success. Where are your success points already? Give yourself credit for what you have already accomplished.

> *Keep in mind, this change of thought does not happen over night, it takes some time to turn things around to a positive way of thinking.*

Jeannette Maw, in her book Pray Rain Journalling, rather than wishing for rain to come, you write as if you are experiencing the rain right now. "Wow, the rain feels so refreshing and cool. I love the cleansing nature of the rain." Writing this way, as if it has already happened calls that experience into reality.

In Leveraging the Universe, by Mike Dooley, he recommends that you spend no more than 5 minutes a day speaking as if its already happened. Otherwise we risk getting obsessive about it.

Chapter 5: How do I have the relationship I want when I'm so afraid of getting hurt?

After I left my first marriage it took me a long time, years, to be ready to date again. I was afraid of getting hurt, being lied to, afraid I wasn't attractive enough. I had to come to terms will all these limitations before I was ready to have this wonderful marriage that I now have.

What relationship do you want to have, exactly?

When I ask this question of clients they often answer with the usual. I want a loving man / woman / companion who is generous and kind, etc. This is a good place to start, however it does not paint the whole picture.

You see we need to be more specific.

When I was looking to meet my husband I put together my Wally Wonderful list. This list consists of non-negotiable, would be nice, and definitely not characteristics. I then used this list to qualify the people I was dating.

It is pretty straight forward.

Non-negotiable's are just that, immoveable, must have's. What do you think a non-negotiable would be for you? Some examples are: employed, capable of deep conversations, funny, healthy, active, etc. If you have the non-negotiable, on your list, that your want your special guy to have a career that he loves you can be on the look out for that particular situation with the guys you are dating.

Would be nice characteristics are the icing on the cake. These could be things like - enjoys sailing, likes to eat out, etc.

Definitely nots are solid markers that if they have this then it is an absolute "No." Some 'definitely not' characteristics that I had, were that my special guy, could not have a bad relationship with money = accumulated lots of debt. He could also not be unkind when you speaks to me and the gifts he brings must be appropriate - meaning what he brings are gifts that I like. Do you see how becoming specific can really help?

I qualify the gifts, to be gifts that I really like, because it's one thing to bring flowers home for me, and it's another to bring Gerbera Daisies (see the specificity here) versus Mum's which I don't like. It's more than the act of bringing flowers home, does he pay attention to what I like?

The flip side is do you empower the men to succeed by telling them what it is that you specifically like?

Do you even know what you specifically like? If not you better get going figuring that out.

Your Wally Wonderful list is important because when you meet someone, it can be very exciting and you can lose sight of the things that are really valuable to you. I hate to say it, but, we settle. We try to see where we fit with this new person. We start to justify, and diminish the things we really want because, at the moment, you really want this partner. The trouble is the 'really wanting this person' wears thin once you get into the relationship and realize this is not the relationship you have dreamed about.

To be really blunt, the person you met is who they are.

Don't expect to change them. If you accept them just as they are, it's unfair to change what you want, later. Stay sharp. Consult your Wally Wonderful list.

When I had this happen to me, I did want the guy and all his characteristics because I had already wished away all the things I really wanted. I wasn't solid on my Non-negotiable's. It was hard on me leaving the relationship and it was hard on him.

Choose wisely.

Your Wally Wonderful list becomes your compass by which you make logical choices about this person you have just met. It really sidesteps the infatuation and lovely emotions that are swirling around when you meet someone new. It puts the rudder of logic into the equation.

For those of you in a long term relationship, is it everything you hoped it would be?

If not, which areas could use some adjustment? What I have learned is that being specific, very specific, in our communications can go a long way to correcting any places that are a bit off. Often we will say that we would like something, however, we don't articulate accurately what that thing is.

Let me give you an example.

You may request that the kitchen be cleaned up when you get home. Cleaning the kitchen could mean any number of things. Is it that the dishwasher be unloaded? Or the counters all be cleaned down, appliances put away and all the frying pans stored in the oven? What is it specifically? The reason specificity is so important is because you want to create the opportunity for success. I believe that the people in your life want you to be pleased with what they contribute.

They want to succeed and help you.

If they clean the kitchen, and in their mind, sweeping the floors and putting the dried dishes away is sufficient, and they neglect to empty the dishwasher, what is the first thing you are going to zone in on? The dishwasher. You aren't even going to notice the clean floors and the empty counter.

Help those around you succeed by being really specific about what you want from them. You will feel pleased because the task has been completed and so will they. They can meet your requirements. Please let them know when they have. This is the other detail we often overlook. Saying thank you, noticing, praising others for good work. It goes a long way to motivating them to continue to do more good work.

If after being really specific with your requests, the other people are not able to remember or follow through, then you may have to consider redefining what you require of them. They may not be willing or able to complete that task. Have a new conversation. Figure out what works for you and them.

Why do you want it?

Why is it that you want a relationship? Have you even stopped to consider this question? Too often we desire what others have because they have it and we do not.

FOMO = the fear of missing out.

Missing out on something you do not really want is not missing out, is it? Taking a moment to consider why you want to have a relationship is an important question.

Let me be clear, I believe that being in relationship with an intimate partner is a wonderful experience and one not to be missed. However, there are times when having a relationship is just not a good idea. If you are entering into a relationship in order to fill a void in you, or to find someone to 'complete you' then I have a few alarm bells going off. If you enter into a relationship with this kind of need then you will be dependent on the other person to supply something continually that will 'supposedly' change you in some way. This is not going to happen. What ever is broken or missing in you needs to be addressed, by you, before you meet anyone.

Repairing and meeting a void in your life is your responsibility, exclusively.

It's your job, I have to put a stress point on this. Being dependent on other people to 'fill us up' will always set us up for disappointment. No one can effectively do this for us in any sustainable way. Everyone else is busy trying to figure themselves out and live their own lives, that there is very little energy left to meet your needs.

Here is another alarm bell. If you find someone who will jump through all your hoops and run circles around you to meet all your needs, you have a big problem. That particular person doesn't have a sense of themselves, they would rather serve you than get to know themselves properly. Now you have the dependency issue going in the opposite direction. It may be nice at first having someone meet all your needs, or so you think. How are you going to feel when they follow you around all the time, text you 20 times in a hour, or check up on you when you are a 15 minutes late coming home? How is that going to feel? That person needs to serve you completely, when you are out or not giving them something to serve they get restless, and nervous. I know this from witnessing it in friends and experiencing it with some early dating experiences.

Why is getting hurt attached to your desire?

So you desire to have a relationship, great! How is it that getting hurt has been attached to this desire? Past experience? Are you familiar with the Law of Attraction? The Law states that what you focus on, what your energy vibrates out, will come back to you. If you are putting mixed messages out, you are going to get mixed back. With the focus on the positive idea of attracting a new relationship into your life, while chasing the idea with "I'm going to get hurt" is never going to work.

You have gotten a couple of things compressed. In order to separate the two, you are going to have to treat the two as separate ideas.

Getting hurt. Where did that come from? Your past? Well this makes a lot of sense.

If you are feeling that you are going to get hurt then there is a hurt in your past that hasn't been healed. What is lingering from your old relationship that has not been healed yet? Let's just say you were cheated on. Your partner had an intimate relationship with someone else while they were in relationship with you. What do you feel because of this event? Take out your journal and dive into this experience. I want you to document the relationship.

Write down the details.

How long were you together, where did you meet, what did

you experience together? Then I want you to consider the hopes and desires that you laid into the foundation of this relationship. What were your hopes, dreams, and wishes for this connection?

Then document the moment you became aware of the infidelity. What changed? What were you thinking? What ideas came rushing into your mind?

The reason I want you to flush out all this stuff is because until you understand and feel the loss of this relationship, and dreams, you will never be able to develop new dreams.

You have to process the emotions from this relationship in order to be ready for a new relationship.

Does that make sense? There is no easy way around this. If this feels too big to dive into on your own, then let me know. I'd be happy to help you. If you need other help I'd be happy to refer you to professional counsellor or psychologist. There is no need for you to do this alone.

Once you resolve the hurt portion of past relationships then your desire can run freely and create the new relationship that you really want. One based on trust, fidelity, dedication, openness, etc. Sounds great doesn't it? It is totally possible for you.

What's the difficult part to see in the hurt?

We talked about the fear of getting hurt in the previous section. If you think about the difficulty that has arisen from the hurt, what would that be? That you can't trust anyone any longer? That you were naive to the deception that was going on? Whatever the residue from this past hurt, you are a different person now because of this experience. You have a new radar that will pick up on things that are amiss.

One of the biggest issues that I see is that people have forgotten how to trust themselves.

If you have been duped once, what will prevent you from being duped again? What on the surface looks like, 'you can't trust others', is actually more about the level of trust you have in yourself.

Early on in the relationship with my husband I had an alarm bell go off.

We were newly dating and I could always reach him by text message. We chatted often. He would respond within a few minutes and no longer than 30 minutes. One afternoon /evening I couldn't reach him at all. I was really curious. My mind never went to "something might have happened to him," rather I was suspicious that something was up. When I asked him about it the next day he said, "I have something to tell you." Oh oh! I was right. What is he going to tell me? I was immediately glad that my intuition was correct, however, I wasn't so sure I wanted to hear what he had to say. He proceeded to tell me that when he met me he was also interviewing two other ladies. Once he got to know me a bit he realized that he really wanted to get to now me more. I could not reach him because he drove to the homes of these other two ladies to let them know, face to face, that he didn't want to pursue the relationship with them.

Pretty honourable.

This guy just went up several notches in my books. It showed me more about his character. I really liked what I saw. What I knew to be true is that he would also treat me with this kind of respect and consideration.

My initial reaction of distrust was completely off the mark.

I could not reach him and something was up, but it was not the infidelity that had my radar on red alert. I was wrong. I had made an incorrect assumption.

I want you to know that most of the time, our assumptions are incorrect. If something is bothering you, check it out. Don't be afraid, especially in the beginning, to have a difficult conversation. It will show you who the other person is. You want to know these things before you commit your heart to them.

I'm thrilled that I was wrong and I'm also proud that I didn't allow my suspicions and uncertainty to run off with me and damage this new relationship.

I am completely accountable for my side of how I relate to others. What I bring, assume, say and mean, are all my responsibility.

Is your desire really your desire?

Often I catch myself getting into the Fear of Missing Out (FOMO) habit of adopting what other people are going for, because I want to keep up, fit in, be important, have something to talk about, etc. When really the goal doesn't belong to me. It's theirs. Have you ever caught yourself in this same position? In the case of relationships, it is often someone else's idea that you have one, or that you have a particular type of relationship.

Everyone means well. They are not living your life, make your own decisions.

Taking an honest look at your desires for relationship means that you get to consciously design and create the relationship that you want.

I met a couple whose relationship still amazes me.

She is a professional violinist with an orchestra. She travels a lot for her work and tends to lean towards classical tastes in her home decor, clothing, food choices, and entertainment. While her husband is an architect who enjoys modern, industrial, hard lines in his home. His preferred home is polished concrete, glass, chrome, etc. You get the picture. Very different tastes.

Early in their relationship they decided that compromise was not something they wanted for either of their lives.

Instead, she lives at her house, travels when she needs to, decorates the way she wants while he has all his own choices within his own home. When I met them they had been married 18+ years and this dual home situation worked really well for them. They would stay with one another, date each other, have their own life - together. It was brilliant. Two happy people, married, living separately, having an amazing life, separately, together.

I share this example because when we look at our desires for relationship the editing process almost immediately follows. Trying to deny your needs and fit into someone else's idea of what a relationship looks like, will never work.

What are your desires for your relationship? How do you know that they are yours? You must run your desires through your own filter, in order to assess how your desires fit with your ideal.

- *What are the things you have heard about relationship from the people around you?*
- *Are there any aspects you admire and would like to adopt for yourself?*
- *Are there any aspects you would like to avoid all together?*

If you haven't guessed yet, I'm an advocate for creating a life you love without compromising yourself. I know this may sound a bit self serving. It is. It is also about authenticity, embrace all aspect of who you are. Which means you really must explore who you are, what you like, what you want to experience, etc. Shakespeare said it well "To thine own self be true."

You may think that embracing all of yourself means that you will be inaccessible to another. This is not true. There is someone who will love you for exactly who you are.

If you do want the relationship what are you willing to give up to have it?

Assuming that, 'yes,' you really do want to have a relationship, then what are you willing to let go of in order to have it? In order to invite in something new, you must make room in your life for that new situation.

Let's take a physical embodiment of the creating space, as an example.

If you are single now, what's the state of your closet? Have you filled it from one end to the other with your things? If someone new were to come into your life, where would their things go? Clear out a portion of your closet in preparation for that new person. Really! Go and take out half of the things you have in there and leave an empty space.

Night stands. How many do you have? Just one? Get another. If you don't have room for two, buy two hanging shelves to mount on either side of the bed. The person you want to attract into your life is going to need room for their things.

Creating this space is always necessary because

maintaining everything you now have in your life leaves no room for someone else to come and share this life with you.

What else are you willing to give up? Some of the easy things to give up are the chores, the financial concerns, the planning of life. You could now share these with someone else. Would you be willing to give up half the chores to have someone come and join you? I bet you would. Giving up something means that the other person has the opportunity to show you who they are, contribute to the relationship and take responsibility for creating with you.

These are the easy things to give up. The more difficult things become your ideas about yourself.

- *Who are you in relationship?*
- *Who do you want to be?*
- *Are you willing to give up some control?*
- *Are you willing to give up on being 'right'?*
- *Are you willing to find a compromise when you'd rather have your way?*

When you are single you get to make all the decisions yourself and have things how you would like them. When this new person comes into your life, it will be necessary to decide how you are going to be with all the decision to be made. If you intend to continue to always have your way then there will be very little room for the other person to be a part of the relationship.

Changing how you think about decisions is so helpful.

Get curious about the other persons point of view. They may disagree with you. Where are you both willing to meet in the middle. A little give and take here and there goes a long way. This is a great exercise to enter into sooner, rather than later. You want to learn how the other person negotiates and how willing they are to find a solution. These early conversations will shine a light on how you both navigate the situation. You can then make an informed decision once you've encountered these other aspects.

You are going to get hurt, so what. So are they.

This idea that you will never get hurt in relationship often stops people from venturing into relationship at all. I have bad news. You are going to hurt. It's unavoidable. Your partner is also going to get hurt.

When you think about it, two people coming together, with all their idiosyncrasies are bound to find some areas of friction. In those moments you both are not going to know how to react or respond. You will often see a part of your characters that are not so attractive. They say something hurtful. They turn away from you. They walk out of the room. All of these reactions may be very hurtful to you. They may raise their voice, go silent, do something unrelated as a result of the disagreement. How are you going to respond to this?

Venturing into a relationship thinking that this will never happen is naive.

It is going to happen.

The important part is how are you going to handle it? And how are they going to handle it? Ideally you want to be able to talk about it and have them agree with you and change their behaviour. The is naive thinking. It may happen that way, however, more often, they are just as committed to their point of view as you are. After all, these are the tools and behaviours that have gotten them through their life so far. This may come as a great disappointment to realize that you are not going to be able to retain all your tools and behaviours from your life either.

What is important, is how the two of you work this out.

My husband tells me that he doesn't care whose right or wrong, he really wants to keep relating to me and finding a way through the difficulty. As do I. My relationship with him is far more important than me being 'right'. This is the nature of commitment. Where is the point that you both can meet and agree? Where can you support one another in your differences?

When conflict happens, the initial reaction covers up something else. The reaction is the release valve that keeps us from the intimacy, the vulnerability and the honesty that are difficult to reveal. What we are really feeling is hard to admit to ourselves, let alone anyone else. We can feel humiliation, at times, or feel unsafe. I would bet that when you have had conflict before, and you have shared openly, it has not gone well, so you don't want to repeat that. Does that sound familiar?

This relationship that you want will be one of the most important relationships, you will have.

If you want a great relationship then finding a way to allow yourself to be vulnerable is going to be key.

The caveat here is that you want to qualify that the person, your potential partner, is someone you want to create that intimacy with. If not, keep your deep intimacies close. Make sure you have the right person in front of you before you do. Sharing deep intimacies is not first date material. You really have to check out how this person is with intimacy by taking smaller vulnerable risks. You do not want to repeat the experience that you previously had.

Returning to love even though there is hurt.

We have covered the fact that you are going to get hurt. They may not intend to hurt you but the result is the same. You are hurt by something that is said or done. This is not the important part. The important part is what are you going to do about it? This is not the other person's 'fault'. They were just being who they are. What is it going to take for you to get back to love? You could choose to hold a grudge, 'get over it' and move on. However, in my experience this is never a fix, it's a glazing over, for sure. It is also an avoidance of conflict. We avoid conflict at all costs. Who wants to bring on a disagreement?

Let me share a huge bit of advice, get into it.

You want to have these conversations with the person you intend to share your life with. Grab your courage and dive in. The only caveat is, you must not make the other person wrong by saying, "You hurt me when you ______." This may be what happened but as soon as you point the finger you are attacking the other person, they will either defend themselves, a natural response, or concede. You can be sure the concession is not given willingly and there is a festering piece of communication that is left behind.

So when you venture into these conversations here is an easy formula to remember. "When you _________, it made me feel ________________ because ________________." The key is that you are keeping the conversation in your perspective.

Here is an example.

"When you <u>used all the coffee cream, neglected to leave a note or go and get more</u>, it made me feel <u>angry</u> because I feel like it's okay to not consider how this is going to impact me."

Do you see how this works? Speak clearly and slowly and keep the emotion out of your voice. This will ensure that the other person is able to hear you. The other person now has a chance to understand how their behaviour affected you.

Keep in mind, this does not mean that they will never use all the cream again.

What it does mean is that you get to speak up when something hurt you. You get to express clearly why you were hurt. This gives the other person the opportunity to understand and choose how they are going to be with this situation next time. This is called being in relationship to one another, relating to each other.

For me, I decided to get over any hurt quickly. It is a conscious decision to find a way past the hurt and get back to love. There are times when I have had to assess if the thing annoying me, say the coffee cream, is really a big deal? It is annoying, for sure, however in the big picture, this loving man who has been nothing but kind, generous and thoughtful to me, used all the cream, once.

So what?

I can get over it because I decide to not make this a part of my relationship. I decide to not make it a big deal. Within the breadth of your relationship this hurt is a minor blip on the horizon. Love is really all there is. When we generate it within ourselves and intentionally share it with others, then we create magic in our relationships.

Intimacy is an essential part of a great relationship, and self intimacy must come first.

My definition of self-intimacy is: in to me see. You are seeing who I am, authentically, when I reveal what I actually think and believe. The areas of my life that cause me pain or that I'm not sure about are the very places that I want to get to know intimately. Those same areas that I avoid are the same places that keep me separate from having what I really want to have in my relationship.

The wonderful thing about doing this self work, knowing ourselves inside and out, is that we don't get tripped up by the surprise memory of something painful, or the recollection of something you are not very proud of. We already know those places. We know where we went wrong and when we have opportunity to experience something similar we can make a new choice.

The other significant benefit of knowing ourselves intimately is that until we acknowledge our darkness we can never fully embrace our lightness. I want more lightness in my life, less depression, less despair, less loneliness, less confusion. All of these emotions, I believe, are caused by pent up situations which have never been resolved. They fester, they brew, and they take root. The self intimacy journey dislodges these old patterns and allows you to understand yourself anew.

For me, my self intimacy began with my journal.

I began writing when I was experiencing a particularly difficult training program, which was emotionally, physically and mentally draining. I was exhausted and starting to fall apart at the seams. I read an article about journalling and thought, how bad could it be? On my lunch hour I walked down and purchased my very first journal which was the start of my journalling journey. I'm now on my 64 journal in my collection. I have written a lot over the years, and restored myself to health through my writing. Through my ranting, crying, raving, despair, depression, and finally to my hope, passion, desire and imagination.

The other important part about self intimacy is that we

cannot love another beyond where we are able to love ourselves.

Deepen your self love and you automatically deepen the level of love that you are able to share. Self love cannot happen without self intimacy.

How can you begin to become self intimate? Allow yourself time alone. Time to be quiet. Time to write, or walk, or meditate, or be in nature. Just be alone.

At first this will be very difficult because our mind chatter is often so active that being alone is challenging.

Teach yourself to acknowledge the thoughts that come into your mind, and let them pass on through.

Allow yourself to practice letting go of the thought. For me, writing it out made it so much easier for me to let it go. It helped me see myself clearly, to understand why I kept getting caught at the very same place. Writing also gave me my history. What I felt on January 1, 2003, is captured forever in my journal. I can look up events and pin point the exact day and entry to reveal my own history.

This has been really valuable when I have second guessed my decisions. I was able to look back at the mental state I was in at the time, what I was thinking, and the factors that went into my initial decision. The looking back helped me settle in and realize I made a good decision after all.

What part of yourself would you rather not see?

In the previous chapter I alluded to the dark areas of our life that we don't want to look at. What are those areas specifically? Perhaps you don't even recall what they are. If you don't have long memories, it could be simply the mechanism in the brain that limits what we remember because it may have been a painful experience. I want to assure you that everything you need to remember is still there and you may remember things in small increments, when it is ready to come out.

So I want you to make a list of all the areas that you think could be a problem. Was it a conflict, a disappointment, a loss, a death, a separation of some sort.

Creating this list is a safe way to collect the events without un-packing them.

Once you have the list compiled then you can come back to it and take one of them to your writing.

Maybe the thing you don't want to look at is something that you have done or said that you regret.

Do you remember when I asked:

- *What it was going to take for you to return to love?*
- *What will it take for you to return to loving yourself?*
- *When are you going to let yourself off the hook for the thing you said, did or experienced?*

This is not an easy question and it may be a bit confrontational. It's meant to be. I want you to get serious about questioning what it's going to take for you to leave these things behind. What is necessary for you to forgive yourself and let these experiences go?

The longer you allow these areas to remain in your life, the longer they hold you back from having as rich a life as you would like to have. Letting go, and creating a new relationship, with any aspect of your life, is your choice, always. However, in my experience the sooner I deal with the things that are lurking, the better off I am. Yes, it takes some courage to face up to where we feel we went wrong. We are human, we are going to make a mistake along the way. Realizing that is part of the release. It is okay, you can begin again.

There are many things about ourselves that we cannot change.

Say your hips, or the colour of your hair, or your height, your width, your nationality. We spend a disproportionate amount of time worrying, avoiding, judging and otherwise turning away from who we are. What a waste of energy! We cannot change these things. The only thing we can change is the way we think about ourselves and the way we relate to these various qualities.

This particular body is all you have been given.

Get to know it well. Embrace all that you have been given because it is yours to cherish and enjoy.

Over the past few years, like 20 or so, I have changed immeasurably. My body shape has changed with age, having a child, various injuries, and the most significant change, is what my heart has done. I'm the same person with a few new grey hairs, I'm a little rounder and softer than I once was, and my heart has grown in it's ability to connect deeply and meaningfully with myself and others. None of this would have been possible had I not spent the time healing the wounds that were causing me emotional and psychological pain. Those wounds were taking up every scrap of my awareness, there simple was no room for empathy, connection, conversation or concern for others.

Chapter 6: How do I believe what people say about me?

Our self perception is often so askew that when we receive a compliment we very quickly whisk it away. This chapter is about stretching to allow these good thoughts to come in.

What have people been saying?

There are basically two types of things people will be saying about you, positive things, or negative things. Both are entirely out of your control.

In the case of compliments, they often come when we least expect it. We may be busy doing something, or focused on completing a conversation. Compliments often come in passing, like an after thought. Which may be a result of how uncomfortable we are giving them. They are often quick and easily missed.

When you received your last compliment, what did they say? Can you recall? Can you feel the truth of what they said? Which aspects are still uncomfortable?

For me, I would receive a compliment, and quickly proceed to negate, turn it around, and otherwise avoid accepting the compliment.

Sound familiar?

In addition, I've been very suspicious about how sincere the compliments are. Many times they were not delivered with sincerity, they don't land as a result. I cannot hear them or receive them. You know the difference, right? When a compliment is genuinely given there is a sweet quality to them, a truth. The ones given out of politeness or obligation are a bit 'off'. Grating on your teeth sort of off, fleeting somehow. Not quite eye contact, just something that is said. You can feel the difference pretty easily.

Our perception and beliefs have a big influence on the compliments that we receive.

If you don't feel worthy of a compliment then it's unlikely that it will land, you will probably discard it. So despite other peoples efforts to express how they feel, you never quite receive the compliment they are giving you. I've heard the saying that the universe has no trouble giving, we have a problem receiving.

Be aware of the gifts and compliments that are coming to you and stretch your ability to receive them. Just this morning I met a client at a coffee shop and she came in and offered to get me something. I declined. Then I quickly realized this is abundance coming to me. Receive. So I leaned over the booth and told her I'd changed my mind. She gladly bought me a coffee. So simple and yet it still needs some awareness.

People are mirrors reflecting back to you your qualities. People are judgmental and whether you have praisers or haters, neither one actually matters. What you think of yourself is the important part. When people are either praising or hating on you they are mirroring back to you the energy that you are giving off. This may be a difficult concept because often we think of things happening to us. That in some way we are victim to the things that happen. You could look at it that way, or you could realize that you have contributed to calling this circumstance into your life and it's now your responsibility to decide how you are going to react to it.

Are you familiar with energy work?

The law of Attraction? If we are feeling grumpy, annoyed, disbelieving or otherwise negative about something then we are attracting those circumstances into our lives. If things are not going the way you planned, figure out how you can change your perspective. Rather than seeing the things happening to you as a reflection of who you are, reset your perspective to: what could I learn form this? Incrementally start to change your mind about the thing that is annoying you. Find something to be grateful for, some aspect of positivity to hold onto and you will immediately begin to attract more positivity into your life. It doesn't mean the thing that is annoying you needs to change, because it doesn't. What needs to change is how you think about it. Once you do change your thoughts then don't be the least bit surprised if the annoying thing also changes. It happens all the time.

Here's the thing about mirrors, they are unbiased. They just reflect what they see. If you are receiving positive feedback, such as a stranger smiling at you, then you are giving out a positive energy. The parking spot in front of the store was available when you pulled up, or you found a $10.00 bill on the sidewalk, then you are giving out a positive energy. These are positive things that you seemingly had nothing to do with. Wrong. You had everything to do with these positive experiences coming into your life. You have been sending out a positive vibe and look what you are getting back.

The opposite is also true.

If your life is filled with things that are challenging you, then I want you to take a close look at how you are feeling about your life. If, for instance, you have a bill coming in that you can't pay, you may be feeling really anxious and worried about it. Then you hop in the car and go to get groceries, which you are nervous about buying because you need the money for that bill. On the way to the store someone cuts you off in traffic and that's the last straw. Before you know it you are yelling and cursing out the driver. All your anxiety and worry caused this reaction. The driver that cut you off wasn't the problem. When you are stuck in worry and anxiety you are drawing all kinds of experiences, like this driver to you. Switch your perspective as fast as you can. What can you be grateful for right now? That the driver didn't hit you, or that you have a store just down the street that you can buy groceries from.

Do whatever it takes to change your mind set. The rest of your day relies on you being able to do this.

What can you see?

What are the elements of your magnificence that you can see? This is important because unless we pause to collect the qualities that you can embrace, you have no way to measure where you are and where you are still heading. Perhaps the elements you can celebrate right now are minor. Maybe there is only one or two things you can connect to. Start where you are, that is the only place we can start from, where we are.

Can you appreciate your hair?
Your body?
Your smile?
You joy?
Your generosity?

Your kindness?
How articulate you are?
What a great friend you are?

These question help establish the foundation for you understanding who you are in the world. It is undeniable proof. I always enjoyed running as a sport because no one could take away the accomplishment that you accumulate. If you ran 5 km then you ran 5 km, it is a foundational accomplishment. What I mean by foundational is we have accomplishments that are solid proof of what we have done. Tangible proof.

So find something, anything, that you can believe and see in yourself. Have you got it? Great! Now I want you to write about what this quality means to you. What is important about this characteristic? Where did this characteristic come from?

The benefit of doing this inquiry is you make this even more solid in your awareness. Once things are solid, our ego, gremlin cannot argue this quality out of our acceptance. For whatever reason our gremlin wants us to believe small thoughts about ourselves, it does not make any sense. The only thing I know is that our gremlin is relentless and unless we develop some skills to deal with it, we will get derailed and become less effective at connecting to this great quality.

Why is seeing this yourself so important? Unless we can see these qualities ourselves then we will never be able to believe when other people are seeing this in us and complimenting it.

What are you unwilling to see?

Contrary to the previous point. What are the things that you are unwilling to see? Believe me there are many qualities that we are not proud of and we try to avoid at all cost. Being judgmental, critical of ourselves and others, irritated, isolating, addictive behaviours, angry outbursts. All these things are less than lovely to look at.

These may be difficult to look at, and it is necessary that you do. These outbursts, habits, and tendencies are running your life, they are typically unconscious reactions. Raising your awareness and consciousness are key to changing these knee jerk reactions.

Why is this even necessary? Because every time you react to life, you are choosing one of the less powerful ways of responding. For example, when isolation and angry outbursts are the reaction, you are drawing more of the same into your life. In addition, you are also putting out negativity that others are then reacting to. Be careful what energy you bring because you influence those around you. I'm not sure you get how much impact you have and the ripple affect of your actions and thoughts. You alone are responsible for creating the life you most want to live and if what you are living now, is not working then it is time to make some changes. We are powerful beyond measure and while we are reacting to the events that present themselves to us, we are missing the whole creative process of consciously creating what we most want to experience.

You may also be unwilling to see the good qualities that you are capable of bringing.

Again this boils down to your belief system and experiences around these qualities. Often we negate what we are inherently good at. It makes us uncomfortable to be seen as good at something. We may be worried that we will be called on to supply this quality ever time it's needed and we don't want that responsibility. If we are known for organizing great parties, we may be asked to organize all the parties. You may not yet realize that you get to say no when you want to. My husband always tells me there are two answers, yes or no, where *'No'* really is a complete sentence.

Once again you get to choreograph your life the way that suits you the best.

All these topics and chapters that I'm putting together for you is for you to realize that you are perfect, embrace who you are and bring your gifts into the light. You will still get to decide how, when and with whom you share yourself fully. Choice, empowering you to live your best life. This is an amazing journey and I'm so happy to help you shine a light on the areas that may still be a bit hidden.

What if your perceptions are off?

The way we perceive the world can be a bit 'off'. I heard a statistic that we are exposed to 11 million bits of information every second and we only retain 50 of those. The best way our brain can manage all this information is to create a narrative, or a story with the 50 bits of information we retain. If you are looking at life through the lens of negativity guess which bits of information you collect - the negative ones.

If you imagine looking at your life through a lens, just like the lens of a camera, you can switch out that lens to see a new view. Your macro lens will show the world in fine details, all focused and precise. Your fish eye lens will show you the 360 degree view of whatever you are looking at. Nothing in fine detail, but the whole range of what you are looking at. The fish eye lens also shows you a distorted view all around the perimeter of the image. Which type of lens are you looking through?

In reality if I am looking through the macro lens I will be aware of every little detail.

It will be easy to see the imperfections and annoyances. It's a *'nit picky'* view with every detail under scrutiny. This is often where petty disagreements live, in the macro view. When you can see the fine details, you can see everything that is wrong, and you can start to fixate on changing these things. This is when nagging, and complaining can begin. There is also a belief that if only this thing changed then my world would be right. Wrong, the thing you are seeing in macro does not need to change for you to be in a better place. You need to get yourself into a better place, then the thing that needs to change will stop being an annoyance.

The wide angle lens view can be a really helpful alternative because you can see the big picture of things and the small details fall away. Some of the things I see in the big picture are that I live in a great place, geographically and physically. The structure and variety of my home, fits us really well. My community has everything that I need. I have great friends close by. I have enough entertainment that I can access easily.

Pulling back to see things from a broader view can really help us let go of fixating on the minute details. Minute details do have their time and place, however, they can feed into a perfectionistic tendency that doesn't move us forward very easily.

Why do you want to adopt what others perceive of you?

Adopting what others think of us, is a habit that we can easily fall into, particularly when the outside view point is negative. When we have not spent time getting to know ourselves intimately we are susceptible to adopting what others think of us. This is because we are living our life from the outside in. We are also striving to improve that outside without taking much of a look at the inside.

This is a habit, it is the normal thing to do, trying to please others and meet their expectations. I guarantee you, meeting others expectations will never bring you long term pleasure or satisfaction, it simply cannot meet your needs. You must meet your own needs first. The reason I speak so strongly about this is because when we rely on outside opinion or circumstances to define who we are, we will be chronically disappointed. The outside world cannot meet our expectations, we must meet our own needs, because only we can truly understand what we actually need.

•

There is also a belief that if I only meet the expectation of others then I will be okay.

Then I will be liked, then I will fit in, then I will be acceptable. This is assuming that you can actually meet those expectation. Too often when we get close to meeting what is needed the goal post gets moved and you run up against unmet expectations all over again, this is a crazy making circus that you need to get out of. So much wasted energy, effort and too frustrating. I think it even verges on abusive.

The reason we want to adopt outside expectations is because it's often easier to understand what is expected of us when someone else if telling or showing us how we need to be. It's much harder to source our own answers, because it makes us uncomfortable. Simply because we are unpracticed at it.

I think trying to meet outside expectation is also so much about our social connections. Our inherent human need to connect and belong. Turning away from trying to meet this may seem like we are choosing to be solitary and antisocial instead. This is not the case, unless you really want that. Once you tune in and meet your own needs, from within, you exude this energy of self acceptance. Self acceptance is a magnetic quality that will attract to you positive connections, conversations and the type of people who get this level of connection.

I think you know the type of person I'm describing. The one that walks into the room and you can feel the confidence. They are inherently attractive because of the clarity that they embody. This is where you are headed.

Is there some truth in what they say, that you resist?

When someone gives you a compliment, and you want to resist it, is there truth in what they are saying? The reverse is also true. In the criticism that you are receiving, that you are resisting, is there truth in it? There might not be any truth in it, however if you are resisting it, there certainly is some truth that would be worthwhile taking a closer look at.

The things we resist are the things we most need to look at.

We resist them because there is something uncomfortable that we would rather avoid. Often it is painful in some way to realize a truth about ourselves. It can also be very frustrating, if we think we have overcome this aspect which is coming to light again.

What is so scary about looking at a truth? It brings up memories of events that are painful. I get it, you lived it once why would you ever want to take a look at it again.

Here is the truth about the situation.

You did live it once, perhaps many years ago, and you now have a new brain and new life experiences that will help you take a look at this afresh. You are not living it all over again, the event has passed, however, it has left a residue with you. That residue is what you are trying to be clear. You could choose not to look at it and continue living your life with this bag full of things you don't want to look at, that would be one choice. With that choice, it takes a tremendous amount of energy to carry that stuff around and even more energy to avoid bumping into it or when you are confronted by it.

Energy is something in short supply nowadays.

With all the activities that we and our families are involved in. I want to conserve as much energy as I can so I have it available for the things that really matter to me.

I guess I've come to realize that carrying around this bag full of things that are uncomfortable is no longer as important, or relevant as it once was. I want to clear things up once and for all, free the wizard, free my brilliance. Brilliance and negative past events cannot co-exist.

What are the things that you would rather resist? Is there a truth there that you would benefit you in taking a look at? Of course there is, dive in, you will not regret it. Go slow and be generous with yourself.

What are you holding on to?

And more importantly why? The things we hold onto are serving us in some significant way, as illogical as that may seem. From my own life the whole story of my adoption, birth family, early sexual abuse, all these details of my life I've been holding onto as a badge of honour. As some sort of justification for how I can't be my 'big', magnificent self.

In reality these were just the crutches that I had chosen to lean on as an excuse not to be my full amazing, wonderful self. Why would I do such a thing? As Marianne Williamson says, we are more afraid of our greatness than our weakness. We are not accustomed to feeling joyful, it feels as uncomfortable as disappointment. Our joy means that we are growing into more of our bigness and we feel, on some level, that we can't take it. It's too much. We are too much.

I'm tearful as I write this.

I'm actually having a tingly body sensation with this thought. I know when I allow myself to dream that my bigness opens up to more abundance and opportunity than I can even imagine. It is like my muse has just arrived with pixie dust to sprinkle me with possibilities. It feels wonderful.

- *What is the badge of honour that you are carrying that has you repeating an old belief about yourself?*
- *What is the story about yourself that you keep repeating?*
- *Is it so well worn in your psyche that you sort of go blank when you tell it?*

What is the thing you are holding on to, as if it is the truth of who you are, I can tell you right now, it is just a story. Yes, you lived it and it is part of your life, but it really has very little to do with you personally. You have not been changed by it, unless you are living into the beliefs you gathering during the experience. Grab some new beliefs, undo the story. I believe the perception of our life is all derived from the stories that we tell ourselves, we make it all up. Why not write a story that has you being awesome and engaged with your life? Let's carry that badge of honour, something that empowers you.

The holding on is a pattern and a habit, it can be a crutch that prevents us from seeing our true selves clearly, you can write a new story, a more empowering story.

If you saw yourself clearly what would you see?

This is where your bigness starts to show up. You are going to need your imagination.

- *What could you imagine for your life if you allowed yourself to dream? You know those dreams that you have that you don't bring out into the light of day.*
- *What are those dreams?*
- *What gets you excited and terrified all at the same time?*

Dreams go hand in hand with desires. We so often negate and diminish the dreams that we have coming to us, because we don't know how to make them come true, or so we think. Your dreams and desires are meant for you, you are the only one getting those specific dreams. When you deny these dreams and desires you are telling the universe, "No thank you". You actually don't get to choreograph the universe. It wants to work with you, but you have to be willing to embrace the gifts you have been given. Otherwise you are living a life that will never be fully complete.

As I write this I find my mind wandering to my own dreams. What I would plan for and have in my life if I allowed myself to really dream, without editing. Often when I start to dream big I allow myself to get distracted before I follow the process through. I'm not an expert at allowing this process to work through me either. However, I'm getting better and better at it.

What helps me to be open to my dreams is allowing them to exist in a light, buoyant, non-attached sort of way.

When I'm not able to be unattached, a dream will come to me, then I will jump to all the things I would have to do to make that dream come true. Which, always, shuts down the dream process, the nasty how to's! I am learning to leave the 'how' of the dream behind. To give room to my dream so that it can expand and grow as necessary without all the figuring and furrowing that the 'how to's' extract.

I want you to take a minute right now to close your eyes and imagine what your life would like if you allowed your dreams to come to life. Calm your mind, relax, feel your body rise and fall with each breath.

- *What is expanding with each breath?*
- *What lightness is coming as you allow this space?*
- *What do you feel? Peacefulness, calm, knowing, or unease in your stomach.*

The uneasiness is telling you that there is excitement underneath.

What is possible from here?

Do you see how this works. In exploring your dreams you connect to all kinds of body sensations that have you feel this opening. Getting comfortable with the change a dream brings to your body is a great way to ground yourself.

This is like a meditation, allow yourself to feel what your body feels, expand that sensation, get comfortable with the expansion. It is a precursor for you living into your dreams.

What would you like to believe about yourself?

If you could choose, which you can, what would you like to believe about yourself? Up until now in this section we have been looking at the evidence of who you are based on the mirrors in your life, your perceptions, etc. I want you to consider what you would like to believe. If you could believe anything about yourself what would you believe? If you were living into your greatness and really stepping into your dreams what would you be believing about yourself?

Here are a few topics that you could choose from.

- *Beautiful*

- *A motivational speaker*
- *A prolific Artist*
- *Smart*
- *Slim, fit and agile*
- *Generous*
- *Kind*
- *An influential leader*
- *A great mom*
- *Accomplished*
- *A wonderful partner*
- *Great with money*
- *Spiritual*
- *Intuitive*
- *Brave*
- *A great friend*
- *Full of new ideas*
- *A genius in problem solving*
- *Resourceful.*

Add a few of your own.

Let's pick one and articulate what they mean to you specifically. Let's say Beautiful. If you thought of yourself as beautiful what would you be doing, saying, or having as a result? For me, I would be eating really good, fresh food. I would be dressing in clothes that make me feel really good. I would be having a luxurious bath every day.

> *These are all things that I would be doing if I were feeling beautiful.*

Once I have this list then I need to make sure these things get scheduled into my day. Do you see how this works?

You move from an idea about who you are, to designing how you are going to be these things in your life, then you will be living into your ideal life. I know it sounds simple and I know that some of these things may take some time and practice. Being able to articulating what it is you see for yourself and then start to make those things happen.

When you do make these things happen, you start to feel the way you want to feel. You have a direct feedback loop to your desire and your good feelings. When we spend time here, creating the life we want, scheduling in the things that are important, we truly do enjoy our lives in a much more intentional way.

If you need any help with this section, or any section for that matter, you can contact me at ciel@ellisinstitute.com.

Chapter 7: Why am I so drawn to my creativity when I have other things to do?

Creativity is a powerful expression and often we do not give it credit. Rather we avoid and wish it away.

This is typical and futile to resist.

Ignore your creativity at your own peril. I'm very passionate about this fact. When your creativity is trying to get your attention, pay attention. I know it means that you have to re-arrange things to make space for it. Do it!!! Each time you negate or ignore your creativity you are throwing away a very important part of yourself. Stop doing it right away, creativity is a blessed gift that is yours to use. There is a quote that says something like

---

" if the voice in your head says you cannot paint, then by all means paint and that voice will be silenced."

Vincent Van Gogh.

Creativity is also the gateway to your imagination, dreams and desires. Our analytical brain is handicapped at doing this. If we are living in our rational brain all the time sorting things out in a linear, methodical way then we are only accessing half of our potential.

You may be thinking why bother creating the things that are coming to me? It's a waste of time and resources. I'll never sell these things, what's the point?

This is your gremlin trying to stop you. Your creative expression is not about becoming Picasso or selling in galleries around the world, even though it could result in that. The goal is, simply, to get you opening up the channels of communication with the creative side of yourself, which is yearning to have a conversation with you. What are you curious about? Let yourself explore what you are curious about. Find a class, take a book out from the library, go on an artists date and explore the textures and materials that you could choose to work with. Allow yourself to be curious and explore what you are interested in. I guarantee it will bring you gifts that you are not aware of.

You may experience resistance, or be frustrated by this exercise and question why you are doing this it all. Get curious about the resistance.

- What is that about?
- Why are you resisting this process so much?
- Is there resistance in other areas of your life?
- Resistance is energy that has become blocked.
- What do you need to do to free up that energy?

Where ever we are resistant there is something that we don't want to look at and consider. Take a look, allow yourself to heal, to express all of who you are even if it appears to be a negative expression. If we never take a look at the negative aspects it will be forever running us from behind the scenes.

What if you discover excitement on your creative adventure? You see a colour or a shape and you feel a bit curious why you are attracted to that item. There is no need to buy and bring it home with you. Take a photo, actually, collect photos of several things that are catching your eye. Then when you get home assemble them in a collage so that you can see them all at once. What is it that you see? Do you see any patterns, or repeated shapes or colours? Get curious about your inspirations.

Do you have any other ideas coming because of this inspiration? Great, allow these creative thoughts to flow and capture them as best you can. Perhaps it's the collage, or you grab a pencil crayon of the colour that you are drawn to and sketch out a shape. Let yourself play, and have fun!

What creative distractions are you having?

What specifically are you being distracted by? Is it an old passion that you have left idle for a while? Or is it something completely new that you want to explore?

If it is something old, that you have left idle for a while, then it's clear that there is unfinished business there for you. Some part of the process that you would still like to explore that never got the chance to express itself when you were doing the thing before. Are you willing to go back and explore that now? There is something that you can learn from going back to that experience. Get curious. What is that part that you would like to express through you?

If it is something new that you are interested in, then what is the new thing that you want to explore? Is it a brand new technique that some other artist inspired you to take a look at? I love this sense of community informing us. Have you ever considered yourself to be a part of that community? If you have been inspired or informed by other's work, then you are also contributing to the community by creating your work from this inspiration.

As an artist you never know what impact you have in the world.

If your work were to inspire someone else to revisit their creativity would that not be a great contribution?

Contribute your creative side to the flavour of life. It will enrich your life and you never know how it will enrich the lives of people around you. There is art within you that wants to express through you, this art can only exist through your hands. You have the power, gifts and responsibility to allow it to express itself.

If you do not answer the call, it's okay, you get to decide. Know that the world will be a little less vibrant without your creation coming to life. It really is ripping off a part of yourself that you have been gifted with and you are ripping off the people who will engage with what you have created. It would be a real shame if you didn't find a way to bring this to life.

If you have the desire what's stopping you?

Desire is a tricky thing, too often we have desires, that we quickly diminish, because we have a belief that it's not okay to want what we want, it's too grand somehow. Just like creativity, your desires are a gift that have been given to you, a gift and a responsibility to find a way to express them.

Desires are the fuel that lead you to your joy, inspiration, fulfillment, and passion. When we negate our desires, we are left with a monotone existing which is sucking the vitality out of us.

Are you feeling tired and despondent in your life? I guarantee there is a desire that is not being met. This is where your imagination comes in. If you could imagine your ideal life or day what would you be putting in your life? What are your desires, with no editing, no rationalizing, nothing to figure out? Let it be what it is, allow your desires to reveal themselves.

Are you still hearing things like: "don't be too big for your britches." "Don't expect too much." "You have to work hard in order to have anything in your life."

I want you to realize something important.

You parents learned from their parents. Two generations ago survival and self sufficiency were still a main focus of living. People gained an education to secure 'their' job and they remained there for the rest of their lives. It is no longer the case for us. For us, we have education and access to information in a way that has never before existed. So if you desire something, then fan the flames of that desire and ignore the neigh sayers who want you to believe things from the past. The antidotes from our parents are just not useful any longer. The world has changed and you are being asked to adjust to those changes. Let go of the past messages that are not working for you, quickly and start figuring out what it is you desire for your life.

What do you believe about being creative?

What are your beliefs about creativity? What are your beliefs about artists? That they are lazy and broke? That they are bohemian, taking from society and giving very little back? What is it exactly that you believe?

Question this belief.

Anything that has you not accept or adopt an open mind toward creativity is a block that is preventing your full expression from coming forward. You were born a creative individual. It is part of your birthright. Again, I'm not suggesting that you create the expectation of being the next Picasso. Be your own version of you with your creative self in full expression. What is the worst that could happen? You make some art, you hang it on the wall, you love it and you have some extra gifts to give away. It can be as easy as that. This whole creative process is not about the finished product. It's about the journey that you will have to travel in order to bring this art to life. It's about the limitations that you are going to bump into, it is about your desires coming to life, your ability to be curious and allow the exploration of those desires.

Julia Cameron in her book The Artist's Way talks about the artist date. This is an adventure that you take yourself on, once a week, alone. You could go to an art supply store, to the beach with your journal, to an open air concert of new age musicians, you could go to the opera. Whatever you are attracted to, allow yourself the opportunity to go and do those things. Once you are on the adventure you pay close attention to what you are attracted to. This is all about observation, attraction, desire, and just playing in the creative arts.

When, and if, the resistance comes up to this practice, ask resistance what it wants to show you.

What is it trying to tell you? That it feels risky to be allowing yourself this time and adventure? It could be more gremlin chatter about it being too much effort. Or it could be about resisting the joy that your gremlin knows you will feel when you pursue this venture. When you are joyful you aren't listening to that gremlin voice, making their job obsolete. They, being the gremlins, like status quo because they get your full attention each and every time you give it to them.

The trick is to make sure you don't give them your attention. Acknowledge them yes, "Oh skepticism, there you are. Nice to hear from you again today. I hope you have a nice day without me because I'm going to the gallery. See ya."

The time you spend learning and growing into this delightful part of yourself is time well spent. Learning how to silence your gremlins is invaluable, managing their chatter is essential.

What if your creativity has something important to show you?

Have you even considered that your creativity has something to show you that you can't get from anywhere else? It does. You can be great at many things, but until you are able to acknowledge and allow your creativity you are still somewhat blocked. I can't tell you exactly what your creativity has to show you. What I do know, for me, is that there is a mood, an energy, a sensualness that comes over me when I tap into my own creativity. I also understand things in a more complete way when I create a representation of my idea visually. There is nowhere else that I can get this sense of ease and flow. It takes an effort to allow this, for sure, but it is getting way easier the more that I get out of my own way.

Around 65% of us, learn visually more quickly than we do from text or auditory direction. So if we are visual learners, what would be available to us if we allowed our visual expression to flourish? Capturing a mood, a memory, an idea in an image may ground the experience in our awareness in a way that simply is not possible any other way.

Creativity is defined by the use of the imagination or

original ideas, especially in the production of an artistic work.

Do you see how the definition of creativity is open to the form in which your artistic pursuit shows up? There are many different ways you can be creative. Dancing, singing, poetry, writing, painting, or music, etc. You get to explore and discover which artistic pursuit you are most curious about. What have you done in the past? What are you curious about now? Where could you experience this practice?

One of my favourite things to do is to walk through the various galleries that we have.

Mainly paintings, however often I run across sculpture, and odd assemblages. The orientation of unusual things always jars my mind into interpreting and understanding this item.

One experience I had, in my effort to understand a particular piece of art work was to sit close by and record the other patrons comments about the piece. What and how were they talking about this particular piece of art work?

I recorded the comments in an endless string, with no punctuation.

It was a monologue generated by strangers all centred around a particular painting. I found it interesting how many people made the same remark, how many walked by, the ones who really stopped to look. It was also interesting to see my own sensations as I interacted in the space with the art and with the other patrons.

As much as I was present, I was silent, and recording. Did the others notice what I was up to? Did I influence them by the very nature of my recording, what they had to say about the piece? I still have the piece of observation art work in my collection.

Take yourself to a gallery or some other art exhibit and see what you experience and see what you are drawn to comment or gather from the experience.

Perhaps you are not solid on your personal progress? Have you ever considered that your creativity keeps coming up because the progress that you are trying to make in your analytical brain is not so solid? This happens often to me, I get jammed in my left brain trying to push, pull or drag and idea into existence and it just will not come. Creativity is the perfect antidote to this jammed up energy. Giving your analytical brain a break and loosening up some ideas in a different realm of your brain is really important. It can shift things a lot more quickly than continuing to jam yourself up against the unknown, unsolvable problem that you are stuck with.

Sometimes confusion and procrastination may show up. These are members of the same team as 'jammed up.' Procrastination has been seen as this bad habit that we use to avoid the things that need to be done. It can be seen as a negative, from outside eyes, that is an easy conclusion to come to, and that may not be the only thing going on.

Procrastination could also be a great place to pause and clarify, gain new insights, even try something else.

When we get jammed there is something that we are missing in the process. Embracing our procrastination and allowing ourselves to shift into a new perspective rather than dragging ourselves to a conclusion that likely will not be the right end anyway, is a lot of heavy lifting.

Confusion is also a tactic that our brains use to get our attention. It can be really frustrating if you don't understand this characteristic. If you are experiencing confusion then it is likely that you don't have enough information. The way to get more information is to stop pushing the same idea and look for extraneous information that can help loosen up your ideas. Creativity is a great way to do that.

Your gremlin may once again be saying: 'This is a waste of time.'

I want you to look at this as a pause, a reprieve, a place to rest for a few minutes and do something else. Change what you are doing and you will see a change in what you are being. There will be a loosening. Spend some time with other things then come back to what you were originally working on and you will experience a difference.

Use your creativity as a productive distraction rather than a criticism.

Your distractions may be trying to tell you something?

While you are working, are you getting distracted? Two things could be going on.

1) *You could have shiny object syndrome which has you chasing the next thing.*
2) *Your distractions could be adding to your creative pursuits.*

How can you tell the difference? How you feel about it is how you can tell.

Shiny object syndrome has you scattered between social media, cooking, cleaning, talking with friends and largely getting very little done. This could be partly boredom, confusion or procrastination. The end result is not much is getting done. On the other hand your distractions could also be ad creative pursuits.

Let me give you an example.

I will sometimes get the idea to call my girlfriend while I'm in the middle of working on something else. If I switch from my work and give her a call I am often surprised by how timely it is to speak to her. Either she is going through something and needs a friend to talk to you, or something she says furthers the work I've been doing. It's quite ironic really.

The lesson from this is be open to receiving new information. It may further what you are working on.

The universe gives us information in unexpected and unusual ways.

When I tune up my receiving senses I can bring in new information from all over. The humming bird that keeps flying by my window, could be simply a distraction or it could be a message. Hummingbirds are symbols for love, rolling with things as they come and joy. What could a hummingbird be bringing me? In a spiritual sense hummingbirds symbolize: Infinity. The fluttering wings of a hummingbird move in the pattern of the infinity symbol. Infinity, eternity and continuity are all associated with the hummingbird. The other prime message is the sweetest nectar is within.

If I apply this new message with the evidence of the hummingbird who keeps distracting me at the window then I am reminded that the continuity of my writing, which is happening at the moment is being acknowledged and supported.

Furthermore, if the sweetest nectar lies within (me) then I'm assured to keep going and share the knowledge that is coming through me. Affirmations from the natural world are pretty cool.

The only way I would receive this from the universe is if I am open to receiving this information in a new way. I am practicing my willingness and openness to receiving all this additional information in whatever way it wants to come to me. It feels really good.

Give this a try yourself, watch what your awareness is drawn to and explore that message you might be receiving. You may find an interesting treasure, like I did.

If you allowed your creativity what would happen?

If you were open to allowing your creativity to flow what might happen? Really, what might happen? Perhaps you would pursue that career that has only been a fading wish. Or you would apply for the job that you think would be great even if your education doesn't meet all the criteria. When you let your creativity flow you take risks that you normally wouldn't take. Those risks yield rewards you can hardly imagine.

I know what you are thinking, taking a risk is dangerous. Only if you see it that way. Taking risks does not have to come with some big consequence that will have lasting implications, it's all just information. You get to decide which risk you want to take and what the possible implications might be.

When we avoid taking informed risk we may be holding a perspective of fear, scarcity or lack.

When we come from a perspective of abundance, nothing is a waste and nothing has consequences that are going to impair us.

Awareness and being at choice is the key.

If you were to let your creativity express itself what would you be most drawn to? Do you still feel a barrier to express it? Pay it no attention, allow yourself to express in the way you are feeling drawn to. This is going to expand you to a whole new level. A new development in how you see yourself, your possibilities and your future.

Less resistance, more love. When you let yourself express what wants to come through you, you are loving yourself. When you give your critic the day off so that you can create, you are loving yourself. When you go to your peaceful place and remove all the pressures of the day, you are loving yourself.

Are you afraid of progressing out of the familiar?

This is a pretty big fear that never really gets addressed. I think it is one fear that actually does hold us back in pretty significant way.

You have worked hard to get where you are. You have spent years accumulating knowledge, things, careers, experience and you have done it all without letting this creative side out. You've done pretty well, you may not see that anything needs to be fixed. There is nothing to fix. Rather it is time to shine, time to have the courage to pull out the red shirt, (or whatever piece of clothing that feels like a bit of a stretch), you know the one, the one that you bought for a special occasion and you've never worn. You keep choosing the things you are comfortable with, choosing the regular. I encourage you to make a new choice, shine, wear the special piece of clothing.

This is a metaphor that refers to your creativity.

It is time to choose creativity over the regular things that you have been choosing. You are going to progress away from the familiar realm that you have become comfortable in, however, it is no more scary that choosing a red shirt from the closet.

Nothing bad is going to happen, there is no need to make any big drastic decisions. You are simply allowing something else to enter your awareness and your activities.

When the time is right, if you do need to make changes, you will know what you need to do. There is no need to panic or worry, allow yourself to progress out of the familiar and see what happens. Course correct as needed, once you are moving, you can always make adjustments.

The unknown is simply that, a state that you have not experienced yet. No more or less scary than the current life you have become accustomed to.

Chapter 8: I was so excited, at first, now I just see obstacles.

This is exactly what happens when our gremlins get ahold of our dreams. It is okay, your excitement is still here, it has just gotten buried by some other thoughts.

What obstacles are you seeing?

The nature of your obstacles can give you some clue to what is really going on. Let's be clear, if you are committed and really desire for a particular thing to come together, then an obstacle is just something you leap over. It doesn't stop you at all.

Let us start there, how committed are you to the thing that you have in mind? If you are committed to a goal that someone else wants for you, out of obligation, then you are going to see obstacles all over the place. These obstacles come up because you are not personally invested in achieving the thing you are setting out to do. On the other hand, if you are committed to achieving what you have in mind then every barrier is going to be removable.

If you are personally committed to achieve something why is it important that you accomplish this? What is your why? Your big why is what will have you overcoming whatever barrier comes up. We often think that will power is enough to get us to our goal. It is not. Will power is not sustainable. However having your sight set on the accomplishment of your goal with your 'why' solidly in place makes the achieving of it so much more likely.

Goals and vision for the future are great, but there is more to achieving your desires than setting a goal.

You must align your feelings and your actions with your desires. It is like a triangle with each side contributing to the whole. You can build a triangle if you don't have all sides together. So your goal will not come together unless your desire, your feelings and your actions are all focused on creating your outcome.

Also, keep in mind that when you set out to achieve something important, fear often comes up. Fear has been said to stand for False, Evidence, Appearing, Real. We believe fear because it knows how to scare the pants off of us. It knows how to get us to not do what we are about to do. Fear's main job is to keep us choosing what we know, the norm. You are rocking the boat, so of course fear is coming up. The closer you are to your goal the bigger the fear is going to get. Acknowledge it and send it out to do something else. Do not do what fear wants you to do. Circle around to why you are doing this in the first place. Connect to your passion, desire, and your bigger why. These are the elements that are necessary for you to achieve what you want.

What other obstacles are you facing?

Doubt, when our confidence is shaky we may use that as the reason to stop. This is your gremlin once again wanting you to stop. I want you to gather up some evidence of what you have accomplished. Evidence, or undeniable proof is solid ground that no one can take away from you. It is a solid foundation to build your dreams on.

- *What evidence is there that you have already succeeded?*
- *What have you already accomplished?*
- *What were the obstacles that you overcame to get to where you are now?*

Write this evidence down and refer to it every time you get a little shaky and your confidence starts to waver.

Have you seen these before?

These obstacles that we have been talking about, where have you seen them before? It is likely you have experienced them before in your life? For me, I wanted to become a commercial goldsmith which meant going to school. The only school I could find in my immediate area was an 8 hour drive from home and they required an art portfolio in order to gain admission. I had never taken art, short of the introductory art lessons in grade school.

This was a big obstacle, or so my inner gremlin would have me believe.

By overcoming this I learned that I am more resourceful than I first imagined. When I have a dream there is a way to make it happen. My belief has a lot to do with the success of my accomplishment. I did get into the art college and went on to train with a German Master Goldsmith for 4 years, quite an accomplishment. I have been a goldsmith for close to 30 years now.

I want you to collect evidence of what you have achieved.

- *Where in your life have you faced a big challenge?*

- *Did you overcome the challenge?*
- *What were the skills that you developed in order to overcome those challenges?*

What I know for sure, you have faced similar challenges before and you overcame the obstacles. You can do it again with this particular challenge.

What we believe we are capable of defines what we will achieve. If you don't think you can then guess what, you won't be able to do it. But on the other hand, if you do believe and can see the positive outcome already, then you can achieve it.

There is a saying that goes "I'll believe it when I see it." It is actually the opposite. "I'll see it when I believe it."

When we take a close look at our beliefs they will tell us a lot about our self esteem, courage, desires and dreams.

- *Where are the loopholes in your beliefs?*
- *Where are the gaps that need to be filled?*
- *Are there things that you believe in a vague sort of way?*
- *What are you looking for to fill in the vagueness?*
- *What clarity do you need?*

What is this obstacle telling you about yourself?

Obstacles can tell us a lot about where we back down. I want to tell you a story about my uncle. Uncle Butch went to the hospital because he was not feeling well. Sort of a chronic cold, low on energy and coughing quite badly. He was admitted for tests, some swabs and samples were taken and sent to the lab. His condition very quickly started to deteriorate. They grew the cultures and were pretty sure they knew what was wrong with him. They began a protocol of treatment with the expectation that he would recover pretty quickly. He did not. He slipped into a coma and his blood oxygen levels were fluctuating into a dangerously low level. The doctors met with us and told us that they are doing everything they can, however, Butch is not responding well. They could not give us a prognosis for his recovery. This was quite shocking as he just had a cough. A few days later, the doctors said that they had done everything they could do and it may be time to start making final arrangements for him. They didn't expect him to live.

I was not going to take this decision as the final decision.

I had also just finished reading a book called Eating Alive by Dr. John Matson, a well know naturopath in our area. I called the naturopath and asked if he would be willing to come and see my uncle.

Perhaps there was an alternative medicine that could help in this situation.

After many discussion the naturopath agreed to come and take a look at the charts and assess my Uncle Butch. The hospital wouldn't release the records to an outside doctor, and the naturopath wouldn't attend if he couldn't see the vital statistics and drug protocols that had already been administered. Back to a stale mate. I'm sure there were some political motivation behind this decision. However, that is a different topic.

My persistence and efforts to locate, and convince him to attend my uncle, had his regular doctors come back to the family with another option. There was an experimental drug that they could try. There were no guarantees. The family agreed they would proceed with this new drug.

They went ahead.

Within 24 hours his vital signs had returned to normal and within 3 days he had regained consciousness.

This obstacle told me that persistence was critical in meeting this favourable end. Backing down was not going to satisfy my determination. I also learned that even if my efforts were not successful, I would know that I had done everything I could to help the situation.

These characteristics of my personality are valuable aspects to know. I can use these to fuel my further decisions. I will do what it takes to meet an end even if it means going up against the head physicians at a major hospital. Authority didn't frighten me, I just kept pushing for a satisfactory resolution.

Do you see how I can now mine these events for the concrete evidence of my character? What are those things? Persistence, dedication, and seeing another option, for sure. You can do the same in your life. What is a circumstance that you would like to use to start mining for your unique qualities? Take some time to look for the qualities you have brought to a challenging circumstance.

Were you really excited or were you trying to prove something?

When we run out of steam perhaps it is because we were putting energy into something that isn't really ours. Meaning that our motivation for working on something comes more from meeting someone else's expectation than it does from meeting our own.

When we are not conscious of the things we are saying yes to, we can often get involved with things that don't fill us up. Then when things get tight and tough we lose all motivation. Why do we get involved with things that we don't really want? I can't say for sure, however, I do know that we are trying to meet a different expectation such as belonging, being liked, sharing our gifts, etc. I know for myself I can say yes to projects because of the social aspect of thing and not really be that interested in the project itself.

Whatever your reason for getting excited about something, if you have lost that excitement, take a closer look at why you were really wanting to get involved. Human nature is such that we all want to belong, to be included, to feel special, like we are contributing something of importance. It can be a bit of a persona that we put on in order to fulfill that role. I'm sure we have all done it, so this is not a bad thing. It's just a process of getting clear about what we are truly motivated for, before we commit to it.

If you committed to something that wasn't fulfilling a social need, then what were you trying to prove?

Were you trying to attract the adoration of your peers by developing something on your own? Why specifically did you lose steam? Did someone say something that had you feel differently about the project?

Whenever you are trying to get your needs met outside of yourself you are susceptible to being disappointed. It's just that simple. You cannot truly get your needs met if you are looking for outside people or circumstances to give it to you. Getting recognition from outside ourselves is a wonderful bonus, but not a good motivation when the project is in process.

Most of my life I was living from the outside in and it never seemed to work out. Many years ago I discovered the way to live from the inside out. It meant being selfish, withdrawing from all my commitments, re-connecting myself with my own intuition and knowing. It was a process of learning to make decision using my own motivation and inspiration versus getting attracted to the perceived adoration and appreciation from others.

Now the spin off may be that you get the admiration and

praise from outside of yourself, however, coming from a place within first, means you are less likely of getting disappointed.

Has your excitement fizzled before? Why?

Have you ever experienced this excitement fizzle before? When, why and with whom? This may be a pattern that you are repeating without being clear that this is a pattern.

For me, and this may sound super selfish, when I am not following my own motivation then things usually fall apart, somewhere along the way. However, when I am guided to do something, even when things get tight, I still keep going. When I make decisions now, I make sure that I check in with my personal motivation. If it isn't a hell yes, then it's a no.

Here is an exercise for you that I learned from Andrea J. Lee, a wonderful coach that I worked with.

Create a three column chart. The left column is Hell Yes, the middle is Maybe and the last column is No. Take a look at all the things you are doing now and file them into one of the three columns. This is a great time to establish what is not working, what is okay and what you are really drawn to. Go ahead, do it right now.........

-Tick, tock, tick, tock.

What did you discover? You have a few things in the No column? These are the things that you want to stop doing immediately. I mean immediately. Call off the plans, back out of the commitment, do whatever it takes to stop engaging with these things. The Maybe list, file these in the No column also. Yup, these are no's as well. If you take a close look you will realize this yourself. They are no's.

The Hell Yes column, hmmm, now we are singing, I mean

heart singing. This is where you want to live all the time. What does your body feel like when you think of living in this area entirely? Excited, scared, all of the above? Good, this is the place of magic.

When you are vibrating at this sort of energy you will attract more of this abundant, joyfulness. At first it may feel a bit intense. That's okay, allow yourself to grow into this energy.

The more you allow yourself to have the life that you really want, the more you will enjoy the life you are living. This is the way to your happiness. That place where you feel fulfilled by what you are doing. Your motivation and energy will be perpetual because it is coming from the well spring of your desire as long as you take good care of yourself. Eat good food, lots of rest, eat your greens, and drink your water. All of these are essential to your well being.

What if your excitement isn't necessary?

What if the things that you want to accomplish in your life do not require that you are excited about them. Let's face it, some things are not exciting, however, you still want to have them. For me, I really love having a neat and tidy house, but I don't get excited about making that happen. I love the result, not so much the work of it. I'm sure I'm not alone in the situation.

Having a clean house makes me feel nurtured and loved. I walk in and feel a sense of calm, luxury and delight.

There are a few ways you can have what you want. You can hire someone to create the clean home for you, you can put your music on and dance around as you get the house keeping done, or you can tidy every day so you aren't left with a big task of cleaning up.

A word about hiring someone, when we give another

person the opportunity to give of their gifts it is an important exchange.

The people that you hire may not particularly love the job either however, they are making a future for their family and you get to contribute to that. Or they may genuinely love keeping house for others which means you are freed up to create your magic. It really is a win/win all the way around. If you feel uncomfortable about having housekeeping help, keep in mind what you are contributing to someone else. Do you see how this works? Your excitement is not essential to you having what it is you really want.

Excitement is a state that is unsustainable. If the energy dips a bit, don't worry, stop fussing!

Instead connect to:
- *your big why;*
- *the people that you are intending to help.*
- *the work in the world that you want to do.*

Your work and contribution is powerful, it will have an impact on many people. So go get the work done.

Where has your dream gone? Is it okay that you have lost touch with it?

You have heard me talk about the macro and the wide angle view on things before. The wide angle lens being the big picture versus the fine detail of the macro camera lens. Where does your dream live?

I feel sometimes that my vision goes from the fine detail to the big picture in a matter of minutes. What I see right now is the micro view of this book getting finished and finally reaching out into the world with the love and intention that I have been holding for all these years.

This dream, writing this book, has faded in and out of my awareness, and yet never really disappeared.

In reality I've known that it has been there and it wasn't ever going to go away, so I'm stepping up and completing on this dream. So whether our dream is front of mind or not, you know it's still there. It never really goes away.

My question is: Does your dream need to be front and centre for you to work on it? I would venture to say that it really doesn't matter. You know what you are dreaming of. You know deep down what it is that you want to create in the world.

The next question is what are you waiting for? There are so many days that go by that are filled with activities that don't really mean much. Each day, if we spend some time working on our dream, we will eventually arrive at the fulfillment of that dream.

Whether your dream is front and centre or not, keep moving towards it. It is still there waiting for you to realize.

If you never find your excitement again for this, then what?

What if your excitement and your dream have really fizzled out? Then what? Then you begin again and create some new dreams. It's that simple. There is no point sitting with what was. It's gone. The train has left and likely that dream has landed with someone else.

I remember Elizabeth Gilbert talking about a book that she started writing, with a very specific location, story line and detail. Soon after she had this idea her life had some big challenges and she lost hold of this story.

When she went back to pick it up, it was gone.

The energy and the inspiration for it had slipped away. A few years later she met another author whom she knew but had never met. Once they got talking they of course were chatting about the books they were working on. The other author told Liz about the book she was currently writing….it was Liz's original book inspiration in almost the exact details. That particular book idea left Liz and landed with someone else.

The lesson here is act on what comes to you and if something happens and you lose a hold of it, let it go because it is meant for someone else. This goes for relationships as well, if someone has left your life, let them go! Holding them will not restore the relationship.

I learned in my leadership training, while working on a very tricky marble maze that each time the marble fell, you simple begin again from the beginning. Gather your concentration, and you start over. There are no consequences, frustration, or worry necessary, simply begin again.

Learning to be light with the things that have left us is essential to moving on with ease. There really is no need to spend any time pining over what was. Let it go and begin again.

Are there really obstacles or just details?

This is a great reframe. What is an obstacle really? It is a challenge, it's a reality that you didn't expect, it's perhaps a time and money drain, however is it really an obstacle or just a detail.

Details will show up as all variations and they may look like: distractions, worry, a detour, etc. What usually happens is that we don't exactly know how to deal with the abrupt interruption, so we try to figure it out, wrestle with it, complain and generally jump up and down with the lack of movement forward. Then we start to worry that we are off track because of t just an obstacle.

How badly do you want this thing to come think about your big picture, wide angle view, your big little hiccup is really that, just an interruption to your p nothing more, nothing less. What are you going to do about it, have a tantrum? That's a waste of time and energy. Simply step over the obstacle, sort out the details and move on. It's easy, once you get the concept that this obstacle is trying to stop you and you get to choose if you are going to let it.

What are you going to choose?

You are resourceful beyond measure, and can figure this out, and find the solution, call in support, back up, assistance, make this happen. If you choose to.

If you change your perspective to the fact that this is just a detail to be sorted, no matter how much it feels daunting, then you will find the solutions. When we ask our brains to be resourceful and find another way, our brains will get to work finding that new way. Being open to a new option means that it is already on its way.

Do you see how this all comes back to your will and your desire. If you hold the perspective that this idea or goal is yours to claim. You are the one with the desire for it. I get pretty passionate about this idea because this is your life, you get to choose what you want to have in it. The time is now so no 'wishy washy'ness', decide and go for it. Get clear on what you really want for your life and do what it takes to reach that goal. Make your life mean something, if even only to you. You don't have to grandstand all over the place. Just know what you want and go for it.

What if the obstacle needs to be a part of your thing?

What if this obstacle is necessary for you to learn what you need to learn? It is going to grow you in a way that you could not grow without it. I've heard that for a caterpillar to make the transition to a butterfly it must do it on its own. If it receives assistance it will never develop the muscle and strength to continue on it's journey. Assistance is what actually killed the butterfly.

In our case, as humans, assistance can be really helpful at the right place and time. As long as the assistance is truly an assistance to us, rather than a directive to move into the ideas of someone else. When we invite others into our process they will always be bringing their perspective, desire and intention with them. As long as they are in alignment with you, then the assistant will work beautifully.

Often though, we are stronger than we think and can actually complete the thing on our own.

Do you believe that you can achieve this? If you said yes to this question, then the answer to the obstacle is also within you. Start inviting that answer in. What are the options that are available for you?

This all boils down to choice, what do you choose to have for your life, to experience for your life, to feel about your life? Danielle LaPorte has created a revolution around feeling our way into the decision that we make for our life. The root of her message is that we have goal setting upside down. We claim our goals based on something that we think we want or need. Yet, there is no guarantee that the goal will actually have you feel the way you want to feel. In her program you decide how you want to feel in all areas of your life, then choose your goals and actions from that place. It really is a very powerful system.

Until we are clear what we want for our lives we really can't make clear decisions. It all gets a bit scrambled and we end up with a semblance of the life that we want. Spending time imagining and dreaming into the life you want, setting a goal based on how you want to feel, taking daily action that has you feel that way, and commit to doing something to move closer to your goal is the key.

Chapter 9: I'm so emotional. Is there something wrong with me?

What do you think? Is there something wrong with you or are you trying to hide your emotions so others won't be disturbed?

Your emotions are only a problem if you think they are?

What have you been told? What have you come to understand about your emotions? What I have come to understand is that my emotions are one of my greatest gifts. I feel things deeply and can express from that deep emotional understanding. Believe me it takes courage to express my emotions, because too often I've been told that my emotions are too much or not appropriate. Sound familiar?

I'm always curious about those that tell me my emotions are too much, because it's not really my emotions that are the problem. It's other peoples inability to understand and be with my emotions that has them want to shut my expression down.

Have you had this same thing happen to you.

I want you to make a mental note of those who have told you that your emotions are wrong or too much. Then realize that your emotions are so uncomfortable for them that they have to do whatever they can to stop you from expressing yours. If I were to ask you, how in touch do you think they are with their emotions, what would you say? I'm guessing you would say, 'not very.' So compassion is a great reflex here, compassion for me, compassion for you. This is not about you or your emotional expression.

If you have people around you who are uncomfortable with your emotional expression, then take your emotions somewhere else. You have the right to express your emotions however you feel fit. The only caveat is that you do it safely and you don't harm anyone or anything in that expression. Freely expressing yourself is a big part of who you are. You emotions are an integral part of your well being, and you have every right to express them.

This whole situation of your emotions being too much works for both sadness and joy, both make people uncomfortable. What I want you to focus on is what are your emotions doing for you? How do you feel when you allow yourself to express openly? Sometimes we feel worse after expressing our emotions. This is normal and natural, let any attachment or judgement go, it is not necessary here. Accept and allow all of who you are.

If you feel worse just after expressing an emotion, know that this will change pretty quickly.

You will pop out of it if you don't allow yourself to judge or connect to what was expressed. It's simply energy moving through you, and your emotions are not the whole truth of who you are.

I will spontaneously burst into tears sometimes. Like the time we were winding our way through the twisted streets of Paris on our way to the Eiffel tower. I wasn't exactly sure when we would see it, the streets were very busy and the buildings were surrounding us. Then all of a sudden we turned the corner and the Tour Eiffel was framed between two multi story Art Nouveau buildings. I burst into tears, stopped dead in my tracks and allowed myself to feel the moment, I will never forget it. I felt so alive, like I was now a part of something ancient, a piece of history that I now get to experience personally. Winding myself into the story of this historic place. Even writing this has me feel all those emotions again. Emotions have a way of connecting us to a time and experience that memory alone cannot. Also our minds cannot tell the difference between feeling the sensations from a memory or feeling the sensation because you are living it in real time.

Who told you your emotions were wrong?

Regardless of who it was, you get to decide if you are going to carry their comments into your psyche. Are you going to believe what they say? What do you believe about your emotions?

There are always going to be people telling us about ourselves, keep in mind that their opinions are coming directly from their perspective. Unfortunately very few people investigate what their perspective is. Examining our own lives takes time and attention, something most people don't make space for.

Those like you and I, are critical contributors to this raising of consciousness. The Dalai Lama said the "The world will be saved by the western woman". I do believe that our clarity, desire, affluence and influence will shift social change in a way that we are unable to measure at this point. The ripple effect of our efforts will contribute to the change that we want to see in the world, keep going.

The things that trigger your emotions are divine moments of connection to something so meaningful to you that it moves your emotions. Our analytical mind cannot trigger this expression.

Rest assured that this is something more powerful than your mind, your spirit is communicating through you, pay attention!

What are you emotional about?

- *When you feel your emotions rising up and showing themselves to you, what are they showing you?*
- *Why do you have tears in your eyes?*
- *Is it from pain or joy?*
- *If you were to ask your emotions what they are trying to tell you, what would they say?*

There is always a meaning coming through our emotions.

In my case, with the Tour Eiffel, the message my emotions were trying to tell me, is: get present with this. You have been dreaming of this moment for such a very long time, be sure you drink in all the details you are witnessing right now, pause and feel this wonderful moment.

Have you ever experienced something great and yet never taken that extra moment to really feel it? I know, we do this all the time, we get a bit uncomfortable and bounce right off the moment onto the next thing.

I want to encourage you to expand your ability to feel into the moments that move you, allowing them to reset the cells of your body to the joy, or the sadness, or the elation that you are feeling.

This is what it takes to heal.

I believe that when we do not pause to feel into these

emotions, which are actually energy in motion, we force that energy to disperse throughout our body. Our cells need to make room to store all this adrenaline, and movement within us. In time, I think that does damage, because our cells are not able to store this immense energy without coming to some deterioration of their own.

When we do allow the energy to flow through us, we create a delicious space of clearing, of acceptance, of expression that enriches our lives all the way down through the cells of our bodies.

Allow yourself to express what is wanting to come through. There is a gift here for you and when you become more comfortable with this expression you also become more comfortable with the emotional expression of others, what a delightful gift. You will become one of those safe places for others to allow their emotions to flow freely. Can you see the potential impact you could have on another?

Are your emotions a crutch of victimhood?

Sometime the expression of our emotions can be to our detriment. Let me give you an example, if and when you have had an emotion that was not acknowledged, usually as a kid, then as an adult you often are still trying to have that emotion acknowledged. This is an unmet need that most adults do not want to be confronted with because it is needy, clingy, and inappropriate most of the time. It can also be seen as selfish and self-centered, which is an easy conclusion to come to when the emotion is expressed in a social setting and it's completely unrelated to current events.

We all know 'that' person who enters the circle of conversation and quickly grabs the conversation and makes it all about them. They are seeking to have a need met from the social interaction and it's often coming from an unhealed wound.

How can you tell if the person stealing the conversation is playing out a victim role?

They have gotten very good at high jacking conversations. They know exactly where to pop in and they often take every opportunity to do so. It comes with a taint of victim, poor me, see me, look I'm important. "See me, someone please see me." You can feel the desperation of it.

You may also have the type who go into moping and sit in the corner bemoaning their poor life. This also has the taint of 'someone please pay attention to me.'

Does this sound like you? It's okay. There is nothing wrong with you. It's just a wound that you need to heal on your own, outside of the social conversations. The social setting has no room to meet your need, it is not the time or place. This is where your journal practice is really important because you can heal yourself, in your journal, on your own, where it is safe to express anything you want. You can see yourself for all the trauma, upset, and difficulties that you have experienced. When you do acknowledge all these things, of and to yourself, you create a space for a lightness and joy to replace the upset.

Once you hit the age of majority, 19, 20 years old you are now an adult and beyond the structure of parenting. It's now your responsibility to give you what you need.

Self love is what is needed.

Ask yourself:

- *What need is unmet?*
- *To be important?*
- *To have someone listen to you?*
- *To think your ideas are great?*
- *Do you think you are important? Of course you are.*
- *Do you have the patients to listen to what you have to say?*

The good news is, there is a very effective way to do this. Journalling! Taking time each day to write about who you are, what you desire, and what needs you have.

I've been writing for over 30 years with 64 journals, to date. I have written out everything that came to mind, I healed myself, I cried myself to sleep, I raged at the things that were causing me pain. I witnessed myself in such a delicious way. There was no one else qualified or available to do that work, it was mine to do all along. Trying to have others do that for me was the demise of many a friendship, I see that now. I will take exquisite care of all of me, so that I can be present to the relationships that I cherish.

I want this for you, to feel this level of connection, love, acceptance and beauty. This is available for you, and the work is yours alone to do.

What else could your emotions be telling you?

Your emotions could also be pointing you to something that you witness that you cannot tolerate. The things that get you upset are the things that go against your values and ideals. This can be a great place to get some direction around where you want to make a difference.

I once had a young mother on the path behind my house abusing her two small boys. I was in the house, on the phone with a client, when all could hear was her yelling at her very small children. I had to interrupt my call and go outside to interrupt her yelling at her children. I did my best to refocus her attention away from the anger, to ask if I could help. I'm not sure how successful I was. Several years later I encountered her again yelling on the street at her youngest child. I wish I could have changed her behaviour towards her children for good. I guess there is a bigger purpose to all this than I am aware of.

The things we cannot tolerate are showing us our values and principles. These are great areas to invest you attention, volunteering or donation your time and efforts in.

Are you faking your emotions? What's the problem.

Where are you using your emotions to manipulate things in your life. Guess what, this is not so productive. You might think this is a good remedy to get what you want in your life. However, this is going to get old really quick and the flip side is that you will not feel very good about yourself. You are damaging your integrity if you are faking what you are feeling.

What is the point really of being inauthentic with your emotions? Are you faking joy when you really don't feel it?

Perhaps you have been feeling depressed for some time so you are going to adopt the 'fake it until you make it' tactic.

It doesn't work, you can only fool yourself for so long.

If you aren't really feeling it, then you aren't feeling it. Each time you 'fake it' you are harming your integrity, which emotionally costs you too much, so stop it. If you are feeling depressed and you put on a happy face and tell everyone you are 'fine,' you are just prolonging the healing that wants to come through you. You may have to create a boundary around this feeling of depression, in order to continue with your work or commitments. You may not have the luxury of wide stretches of time to sort this out, on your own. It's okay, take small steps.

I've heard that depression is a reaction to suppressed anger. I can't recall where I heard that, yet it seems to make sense to me. In your private journalling time, explore any hidden angers that you may have and ask them to reveal what you are meant to learn from them. This will help ease the depression.

If your depression is chronic and you feel you are unable to function then please, consult with an expert. Call a counsellor, psychologist, or help line to talk this through. There is no need to suffer in silence.

Your emotions are just for you; and people you trust.

Do you remember how I pointed out that your emotions are yours alone to heal. Consider at some point, you may want to create a deeper connection with someone else, which means your emotions are coming along with you. How do you reveal your emotions to someone you want a deeper connection with, without using your emotions for sympathy? You must do this carefully. Keep in mind your deep truths are not to be revealed to a brand new acquaintance. There is a bit of finesse with this. Reveal a little more of yourself each time. Monitor what happens in the other person. Are they able to come forward with an intimacy of their own?

The tendency can be to rush forward and reveal all kinds of things at once, please do not. It rarely creates connection when we unload our emotions on a new relationship.

I caution you against revealing too much, too soon, because it can be quite intoxicating to have a sympathetic ear and you may lose sight of how it's impacting the other person.

Go slow.

This is a give and take sort of connection, reveal a little bit of emotion, monitor how it is received and is the intimacy reciprocal? Does the other person reveal a little bit more about themselves in return? If they do come forward with intimacies of their own then you are starting to build trust in your relations to each other.

If the intimacy is not reciprocal then you get to make a new decision.

Is this the person that I want to be building more intimacy with? You really don't want to reveal all your treasured things to someone who is just going to run with them and never share anything of themselves.

You also have to be careful that the person you are building intimacy with will keep that intimacy between the two of you. Often times the other person may have a tendency to talk about the things you have discussed, breaking your confidentiality, which is not helpful or trustworthy.

Before you reveal the really important parts of yourself watch what they do with the easier things to share. If they break your confidentiality, then you know not to share the deeper, more meaningful things with them.

What if your worst emotion was actually your clearest friend?

You know the really big emotion that you keep avoiding, like your rage. What if it is your greatest ally? How do we deal with it? You bring it out and have fun with it, allow it room to play, in a safe way, and express it in any way you feel called to.

Here are some suggestions.

- *Go to a brick wall somewhere and smash some china - amazing!*
- *Go to the rocky shore line and throw things.*
- *Take a sharpie marker to that rocky shore line and write on the rocks what you are so fearful about, then with voice - sound of any sort, throw them with passion into the water.*

- *Get a baseball bat and beat your pillows as a way of expressing your anger.*
- *Jump up and down while screaming at the top of your lungs.*
- *Park your car somewhere in a secluded place and with the windows up, scream as loud as you can.*

These are all great ways to give a release to the rage that is running within you. Keep in mind releasing this big emotion is really good for your health, as long as you do it in a respectful way. In a way that doesn't hurt you or anyone else.

When your rage comes up and you allow yourself to express it, you will feel a release like nothing that you have ever experienced before.

A number of years ago, I did this exercise with a set of china that my mom had given me.

It was the first set of fine dishes that she received from her mother in law when she got married. It was not an expensive set and in fact the plates had become all crazed with cracks that were turning dark. They were wearing out, which helped me justify smashing every single one of them. The relationship with my mom had been one that was never as deep as I would have liked. I have come to realize that I was expecting a level of intimacy that she was not willing or able to give. Needless to say at the time I was so angry I needed to do something, so I took the dishes to a concrete wall and proceeded to smash every single one. It felt so good and so wrong all at the same time. I was sure that someone was going to come around the corner and stop me. The sound of shattering china was shocking.

Flinging the turkey platter, that was epic, like a big heavy frisbee.

P.S. I cleaned up all the debris and threw everything out.

What I learned from this exercise is that there was so much energy and anger pent up that just would not release without this physical exertion. The sounds of the destruction also helped me release the things I had stored up.

This smashing of china was so cathartic. I was breaking the social standard of protecting the china, and creating a sound that strikes fear in everyone doing dishes after Turkey dinner. Give it a try if you are having big emotions coming up that you don't know what else to do with.

Bring on the emotion.

As you can clearly tell I'm not the least bit intimidated by my emotions, large or small. I've learned how to express them and the people around me are people who have an appreciation for my vulnerability, authenticity and consistency.

My husband said, as I was crying away about something, that he loves all of me just the way I am. Don't change a single thing. He loves how deeply I feel things. What a refreshing treat to have people in my life who support me in my emotional connections. I planned this, honestly. When I was looking to get married again I wrote about, prayed about, and watched for that man who could hold the emotions that I feel. I found it in this man, I am so grateful.

You have more choices than maybe you realize and if someone shows you who they are, believe them. I think that was Maya Angelou who said that. My husband showed me that he could hold me in all my emotions. I in turn was thrilled that I had finally found someone who would accept all of me. It was a win, win situation.

Do you have someone in your life that can be with all your emotions? If not, take some risks and see if you can find that person. When you find them, they also find you. It's likely they haven't had someone who can support their emotions either. Being at our best, accepting all of who we are, gives other people the opportunity and encouragement to accept all of themselves. This is the ripple effect that I have been talking about. You have an impact on the people around you simply by being your best.

Who do you attract when you are emotional? Your 'people'?

Like I was alluding to before, when you are emotional you allow, encourage others to be emotional. If you are in business, then guess what, your emotions attract your 'people,' the people that you most want to work with will be attracted to your vulnerability and emotion. I'm also referring to this attraction factor in your unspoken intention and energy. I'm not suggesting that you should be gushing, with all your emotions, on that new client. What I am saying is that when you are aligned with the clarity and beauty of all of you, it shines in the work that you do. It's unspoken and they can feel it, you will be attracting people to you versus persuading them to come and work with you. Attracting is always so much sweeter than pursuing the connection.

The other cool thing about attracting your tribe is that you get to have more fun, more deep conversations and grow into more expressions. It's perpetual and feeds off itself.

I don't think you can imagine how refreshing it is to find a group of like minded people to engage with, where everything is welcome in a community of safety and connection.

It's a beautiful thing.

I think it is how we are meant to interact.

When you create this with your tribe, again you create a ripple of connection with others whom you may not even know. The people you connect well with will take what they have learned from you to their people. The ripple will be created in their circle also.

I'm not sure if you realized this yet, but by sharing this book with you, I am leading you to become the best version of yourself, so that you can create the influence that you want in your circles. "Hee, hee, hee," as she cackles with a sneaky grin.

This was always my master plan. To live my life with the pursuit of healing myself and using my experience to help others heal. It's a pretty cool place to be.

Here is my leadership piece in the world.

> "To teach people how to reframe the stories of their lives in order to remind them of their love, passion, and power and then to use those elements for inclusion rather than exclusion."

What is your piece of leadership in the world? Give it some thought. You have a very unique gift to share.

Chapter 10: How do I engage my dreams? It's been so long.

Dreams are fluid. They continue flowing whether you have connected in a while or not. Tap in, get still and listen to what your intuition is telling you.

Dreams are great because you can always begin again. I talked about this a little bit earlier in the book. Our dreams are not set in stone, we are free to choose a new one, if we wish. Some dreams will lie in wait for a very long time, until the moment is right to be realized. Other dreams come and go without consequence. You get to create the life you want to lead, which means, if you have some old dreams, pull them out and see if they are still current, do they still have merit, or are they tired and need to be let go?

Dreams and desires live very close to one another, and both require that you get still and listen for what is needed next. Listening is a big part of connecting to your dreams, as is feeling what your dreams feel like. Where in your body do you feel your dream?

For me, there is an effervescence that comes up from my belly.

It is blue in colour and like thick soapy bubbles of love and joy. They expand and well up, bringing delight into my chest and will often make me giggle.

- *Can you describe what your dream feels like?*
- *What colour is it?*
- *What texture?*
- *What temperature?*
- *How does it move?*
- *Where does it begin and where does it travel to?*

When we apply the senses to our descriptions it roots the awareness for us and becomes more tangible and tactile. We can then assess, when a feeling comes up, is it the same, or different? You can start to discern which ones are the most engaging by the level of feeling that gets stirred up, by them. It is a great measurement point for our desires and dreams.

Now, here's the thing about measuring,

if we are measuring we can recognize the change for better or worse.

The other benefit of measurement is that when we are about to make a decision on something, check in with this part of yourself and see what it feels like. If it does not hit the key measurement points, that you know to be the expression of your dream, then it's not the right fit for you, it's not your dream and you can let it go.

Tap into your feeling self again and see what comes to you concerning this opportunity. Is there a version of this that would fit better? Or is your dream about something else entirely? Use these touchstone sensations to determine how you are going to respond.

Are you suffering dream fatigue?

Dream fatigue is when you have set out to make a dream a reality, and more than once they have fizzled before being realized. We put an effort in, we put our hopes on things, and when they fall through we can feel fatigued and upset. I get it, it is exhausting to set out to achieve something and not have it come together.

The other thing we often do is pile on several dreams, at the same time, which makes it difficult to focus on any one of them. In essence it fractures our ability to manifest even one of them, so stop this habit, if this is a pattern for you.

The other thing with having many dreams at once, is that you get personally confused.

You really need to pick something, focus on it until it comes into view. This is not to say that having a plan of growth is a bad idea, because it is a great idea to envision the big picture, but then scale your big dream into small pieces that you can easily focus on. That is where your success is going to happen.

Dream fatigue is a terrible place to be, it is a wasteland of creative inspiration gone wrong. All hope and joy have left because you are exhausted from your efforts. Give yourself a break and do not embrace anything else until you feel better. Do whatever it takes to feel better. Do you know what the practices are that will have you feel better?

If not, this is your first thing to figure out. I want you to make a list of the things that will have you feel better.

- *Perhaps going for a walk,*

- *taking a bath,*
- *calling a good friend,*
- *spending some time in nature.*

Go and explore some of these activities, paying close attention to which ones have you feel better. Record them on your go to list and make a point of scheduling these things in.

You must get yourself feeling better before you set any more goals. A mentor of mine Sandi Amorim reminded us that you cannot create anything good from negative energy. Do whatever it takes to get your energy feeling better, then make plans from there.

Dreams can be so demanding.

Dreams require that we be focused and intentional with our actions. It is when our thoughts, feelings and actions align that we accomplish the things we want to.

At the same time, it is essential to stay loose. It seems like a contradiction, however, our dreams can come to us in many ways, ways that we may not expect, stay open.

Dreams also require our commitment, our willingness to keep showing up and dedication to move them forward.

In the past, I have set many a goal and stopped myself before I ever got to the goal. Why did I stop? I let fear get in the way, I got scared, I got busy doing other things instead. Hello saboteurs you are sneaky and really effective.

For me, this all changed when I got tired of setting out to accomplish things and never reaching them.

It has taken getting fed up with my way of working to finally get committed and do the work. There are no shortcuts. The 5 steps, or 10 steps to the 7 figure income in 10 minutes of less a day is just not true. You have to show up and do the work.

The other thing that has changed is that I have found a community of like minded people who are creating amazing things. We support one another. Together we can make anything happen. It has been so valuable having the support and supporting others, as they reach their dreams.

What can we do when our dream seems to be demanding too much of us? Break it down into smaller bits of the larger dream, nothing needs to come instantly. Break things down into manageable pieces so that you avoid that feeling of overwhelm.

Dreams are supposed to light us up, however when we create overwhelming or short deadlines, we weigh them down with such heavy expectations they become a chore to realize. Lighten up, stretch the time line, give yourself some breathing room and enjoy the process!

What brings you alive? Would you like more of that?

Do you know what brings you alive? This goes back to your feel better list. Are there things on that list that have you feel alive? When you are alive, it is like you are floating though life, inspired and engaged in what you are doing.

Here are some questions to help you reflect on what gets you excited.

- *When were you last inspired by something or someone?*
- *What was going on?*
- *Who were you with?*
- *What exactly were you feeling?*
- *Would you say you were feeling alive?*
- *What if you could have more of that sensation in your life?*

- *Would that be good?*

You can bring that sensation into your day any time you choose. You have it in your memory, so pull it out when you are feeling a little less than alive. Pull it out and take yourself back to that sensation, feel it in your body. Make sure you feel good, damn good, before you work on your project because your results depend on it.

You have more control than I think you realize. Use this skill that you have to shift the energy of your day and your awareness.

Music is another great way to shift the energy, it can elevate your mood beyond the moment. Shift the energy and get you into a more alive state of mind. Dancing is also another aspect of shifting your energy. Anything that gets your body, mind and soul moved from the ordinary to the more elevated state is perfect.

When you don't feel good, choose one of your go to things and allow yourself to feel better. Then return to your work. Your results will always reflect this shift in energy.

Dreams seem so final what if something better is coming?

Do you ever get this? When you set a dream in motion it requires that you commit to it. But how can you commit when something better may be coming? It is quite a dilemma. You need not give it much attention because if you are setting your intention and holding the goal lightly then you can always course correct when you feel it is necessary.

The only thing that really stops our dreams is us. We talk ourselves out of our dreams and goals because they don't look the way we expected, or they don't come together as quickly as we thought, or we hear something detrimental to our progress, or we get busy and switch to doing something else.

Commit to what you want, stay the course, adjust your direction if you are getting a bit off track and remember you can always begin again.

The reason I'm encouraging you to do all of this has nothing to do with your dream.

I don't really care about the dream you set your mind to.

What I do care about is that you follow through with what you say you are going to do. It is way more important to follow through with the commitments that we make to ourselves, it is our integrity that is at stake, if we do not. If you are losing integrity with yourself, you are also losing integrity with the other areas of your life.

You integrity, is something you cannot live without.

You can't live well, anyway. Once you have lost integrity with yourself it is very difficult to get it back. You don't trust that you will follow through with what you say you will.

The only way back from this situation is to begin again. Start with a small commitment, something you are sure that you can follow through with and make sure that you do.

I don't even care what you commit to, it could be taking a nap each day, just make sure you follow through. Make it the number one priority, make your commitments mean something to you and make sure you keep your word. This habit will do more for your success than any level of acknowledgment from others.

What do you value?

Do you know what you value? Values do not generally change throughout the course of your lifetime. If you value honesty you are not going to devalue it along the way. Some typical values are: adventure, beauty, contribution, creativity, discovery, feelings, pleasure, etc.

Needs on the other hand do change over our lifetime, as we mature we need different things. For example you may have the need for being loved. Once you decide and explore the process of loving yourself, then that need has been met. You can move onto a need such as freedom, or connection, or acceptance.

My values include: Emotions / Feelings; Teaching; Catalyst; Sensitivity; Contribution / Creativity. These values are non negotiable. They are listed in here in the order of importance. I live my life through my feelings first which gets expressed in my teaching which encourages me to be a catalyst for other women. My Sensitive and creative contributions make a marked difference in the world.

Let me tell you if I do not place a high priority on these things, I go off the rails.

I get depressed, disorganized, despondent, scattered, unsure of myself, basically my life turns into a train wreck. Then I get the 'pleasure' of cleaning up the mess that I got myself into.

I encourage you to figure out what your values are.

It you would like some help doing that, get in touch with me. We can easily step in and get this done together. ciel@ellisinstitute.com

Once you have your values established then consult them each and every time you are developing a plan for your life. When you are setting your goals, consider that you want these things to be a part of it.

When I honour my values by considering them in my commitments, I feel happy that I have made the choice. I feel happy that I get to play in this realm of creation. My life runs smoother, I appreciate the things I encounter, and I honour the gifts that I have been given, it is a win, win situation.

Seekers keep adjusting the destination - to keep it interesting

Seekers, do you know what I mean when I say that? Seekers are those among us who are seemingly never happy with where they are, not in a bad way, just always wanting to learn and explore what is possible from each new place.

Appreciating where we are and what we have accomplished is an important piece and yet seekers always want to keep going. It is really interesting to keep expanding who we are, trying new things, evolving.

I'm excited about this prospect because never before have we had this much freedom to create the life that we want to live and more importantly to influence the world that we live in.

If there is something not working, perhaps you are a seeker as well. Perhaps you are a seeker who has lost the vision of facing forward. You are not obligated to stay exactly where you are. You have many options such as reading about some new ideas, take on a new hobby, etc.

Seekers take risk and try new things, while engaging in the things that have meaning to them.

Where are you on the spectrum of seeking the life that you want to live?

There is no judgement here, rather an observation, nothing is wrong with you and there is nothing that needs to be 'fixed'.

If you are reading this book then you are looking to let something go so that you can live more of what you want. So what is that thing that you are seeking?

There is no wrong way to figure your life out. You create the experiences of your life, so why not decide what it is that you would really like to have and go get it.

What are your sleeping dreams telling you?

Now I'm no expert at sleeping dreams. I have done very little analysis of the dreams that I have. What I do know is that recurring dreams are showing you something. Our daytime and nighttime dreams are not here to scare us, they are your subconscious minds way of showing you things that you may need to take into consideration.

The main message here is to embrace the life that you are drawn to create.

It is yours to create with your life purpose, discovering what brings you alive and experiencing more of those things.

What I know, from my own search for 'my' life, is that you are a divine creation with unique qualities and attributes. Your life consists of opportunities to explore those gifts, to shine your light into this world, bringing joy and delight to those who know you. What are you waiting for? What scares you about this possibility? Whatever you do, do not let fear be the guide of what you do with your life. It will always end you up in the ditch, always! It will keep you in a safe little container never exploring what you are really capable of.

Use your dreams to inspire you, and let them ignite curiosity and excitement. Then find ways to live into those moments of inspiration every chance you get.

Chapter 11: How do I take care of myself when I'm so focused on this thing?

Have you ever had this happen? You get focused in one area of your life and all the other areas fall apart. I've been there too.

What does taking care of yourself really mean?

I think by this point you have a pretty good idea what taking care of yourself means. If not, then you certainly know what not taking care of yourself is like. Where is your awareness around self care? Many of us, myself included, got caught up in the busyness of life, raising a child, going to school, etc and lost sight of what I needed to be well, myself. It was a pretty desolate place for me. Drinking way too much coffee, not eating properly, staying up late in order to get university projects done. Those days are over for me, I no longer push myself so hard. I also have remarried and have some additional support which always helps to get things moving smoothly.

Single or not, taking good care of ourselves is very important.

I'm not telling you anything that you don't already know. What is confusing is that there are so many contradictory ideas of what taking care of yourself means.

What I have come to learn is that taking care of myself is an inside job, I get to decide.

I get to try some things and see if I feel taken care of. If I don't then I let those things go. I have bought many different memberships to yoga studios, salt water float tanks, gyms, etc and once I was oriented into their space, soon realized that this does not work for me. I don't enjoy the structure, routine, and environment of these places. So I cancelled the memberships, left their routine and have sought out my own routine.

Self care takes dedication and commitment. Our dreams, desire, self care all come back to our daily practices.

At the core, my desire, with all this writing, work, adjustments, care and attention, is designing and living a life that I love. To live with all of my passion, personality, and purpose rolled into one glorious bundle. This is not a selfish pursuit because when you are living a great life you are better at sharing your inspired living with others. You create a change in the world and community that is for the positive.

Maybe this thing needs all of you - for now.

There are times, like right now, that my thing - this book, is requiring all that I have available. There are going to be times in your own life that your total dedication and focus is going to be needed to accomplish what you are setting out to do. Just know it is temporary and jammies are appropriate day time clothes when you are immersed in the creation process. Let the expectation fall away and allow yourself to be in the creative cocoon that will have you succeed. Just for now, let yourself draw in and create what you want.

This is an important reminder because too often we try to maintain everything that we have going on which overloads our ability to get any one thing done. Give your people notice that you are diving into an intense creative time. Ask for the help that you need to get meals on the table, or the pets looked after, or the groceries bought. If you are on your own, then order in take out, Let the dishes sit. Do whatever it takes to get your thing out into the world.

You can do this for short periods of time and still resume your routine once you have completed your project. The trick is the resuming part.

Maybe, just maybe, this thing you are working on is going to take everything you have to bring into existence. Dedicate to it and make it happen, go hard, go harder, until you see this thing through, this is the realm of champions. Going the extra mile to make sure you don't let yourself down.

Who could support taking care of you?

Who are the members of your pit crew? Who could you call in for assistance? Who is your back up? We all have people waiting in the wings who want to help us. I know you are a person who likes to do everything yourself. I get it. You feel strong and capable if you are doing it all yourself. You may feel the satisfaction of being personally resourceful. Keep in mind, there are others around you who want and need to help. When you allow someone else to help you, you give them a gift of assisting. I really have to stress this point because muscling though on our own is fine. We can do that, however, easing our load and allowing others to assist, draws on their talents, builds connection, generates a feel good feeling in them for the honour of assisting your idea. It is a service to your creation to allow others in. Be generous, share in the good that you are creating, by allowing others to sneak in and feel some of your excitement.

Ask yourself, who would cook you a meal and bring it over?

Who would sit with you while you shared a meal with them and listen to your process? It may help you with the last pieces of your idea.

Who could pick up your kids so you can stay home and complete on your project? People rarely mind doing this because they know one day if they need the same from you that you will reciprocate. It is like having an I.O.U., that can be called up when needed, it feels good.

Who would help you get the word out about the thing that you are creating? Who has a network of people that would like to hear about what you are working on? They could promote for you and you could promote for them, reciprocity.

This is where things get fun, you get to see the people around you rallying to help because they believe in the things that you are working on. You get to see the joy this project is already bringing, which fuels more joy circulating around. It is a delightful circle to be caught in.

Are we talking major neglect or just hygiene issues?

Where is your level of self care right now? Is it minor things like I need to wash my hair or brush my teeth, or is it major neglect? I ask this with no judgment. I am curious about the degree to which you are neglecting the very sacred vessel, of this body and mind, that you have been given.

Self loathing and self neglect, from my experience, comes from past pain and an incorrect self perception. These are learned behaviours from the experiences of our lives, no judgment, all compassion, compassion for you and compassion for me. If you are neglecting yourself as a habit, then I want you to stop that habit, immediately. The way you stop is you do one small thing that you define as self care. What would that be, brushing your teeth regularly, flossing, having a shower or bath everyday, taking yourself for a walk around your neighbourhood, talking to a friend? Begin here. Begin to design your self care in a way that has you feel better. Start acting differently with yourself and you will start to undo the experiences of the past.

Ask for help, find someone you can talk to about how you are feeling.

You may need a professional, and there is nothing wrong with that. Whatever you do, choose someone who is healthier than you are. Someone who is non judgemental, who already knows you and wants to help you.

If you are on the other spectrum of self care where you are experiencing minor neglect, then stop it. You know what you need to do to take good care of yourself, go and do those things, you are important.

Your self care is the foundation of your well being.

You cannot expect to live an empowered life if you are unwilling to take care of this beautiful body that you have been given. I know you have all these things that you cannot accept. The size of your calves, thighs, hips, boobs, your flabby arms, your double chin. The list goes on. Guess what? Hating these parts of yourself is a waste of energy. You cannot change it, until you are willing to take good care of yourself. Your genetics have dictated the shape that you are and baby you were made that way, stop fighting it. Accept that you were born magnificent and stop wasting time grimacing over the things that you cannot change.

Peripheral vision can be really helpful to widen our view.

When we are working intently on one specific thing in our life, our self care can very easily become secondary. This only makes sense because as our view narrows and we dive in deeper to our project, our peripheral vision becomes dimmed. Peripheral vision doesn't actually require a change of state. You can stay focused on the project, but retract your eyes for just a second and become aware of the things that are in your periphery. What are you aware of? Temperature, light, smell, order? All of these things are in coexistence with you at this very time. Self care can include the attention to these details which will address a self care that is within your immediate reach. For me, it is the plants that need to be watered. These plants fill my space with flowers and energy. They clean the air and remind me that I am alive, like they are alive. So in my periphery I'm aware that these plants need attention, which is actually a facet of my own self care. When I care for the things that are living in my space then I'm also taking care of me.

Peripheral vision can also show you the things that you don't easily see with your regular vision.

Perhaps there is a clutter accumulating in the corner that you have become blind to. Perhaps there is dirt and dust that is swirling in the corners as you work on this project.

When our spaces are clear we allow room to create something new, with a space that supports that creative processes.

Take a moment to allow yourself the distraction and tidy up the periphery of what you are aware of. It will change what you are able to accomplish when you come back to the work.

Are the other 'taking care' of you things dead weight?

Do you know what I mean when I say the other taking care of things? These are the things that you have put in place somewhere along the way, but have not considered since. These are the routine things that you have not checked if they are still supporting you. The routine way of acting and doing things in our lives, which has become unconscious.

Well, it is high time you took a look at the other taking care of things because if you are to design a really great life, a life that you love, all these unconscious things need to be assessed for their value. If they are marginally valuable then they are not strong enough to remain in your awareness,

let them go.

One way you can make these assessments is to grade each thing on the level of satisfaction and 'feel goodness' they bring you. Make a list of the things that you are currently engaged in during your week. Pull out your daytimer and list the various categories of activities that you are part of and give them a level of satisfaction from 1-10. (10 being a lot and 1 being not that much.)

Keep in mind some of the thing may not be able to move, even if you are not satisfied with them. For instance Johnny's 6 am hockey practice. That is a non-negotiable, because in order for him to attend and develop his skills, the 6 am practice is necessary. The challenge then becomes to develop a new relationship with this early morning commitment. You could establish what is good about this practice. Even though it is a challenge to get up early and make this happen, you can focus on the bigger why of this commitment.

You could even dedicate the 6 am time, when he is practicing, to something that would benefit you.

Perhaps bring your journal along, or grab a coffee and snuggle in for the hour. What other things could you use the early time for?

In the realm of the things that you can change. Which ones are dead weight and not serving you any longer? Having a regular coffee date with a friend. It used to be a great place to connect and engage. However, the enjoyment of your time with her has dropped off. So what would you like to do about it? Perhaps seeing them every two weeks would clear up some space in your schedule and still keep the connection. You always have options, as long as you are willing to rearrange things, try something out, and be open to re-creating something amazing.

Who are you competing with?

You may not think of this as self care right away, however, this certainly is self care. Jealousy, envy, and / or comparison are all versions of the same competition mind set. If we are living our lives in these realms then we are coming from the 'not enough' perspective that we carry inside of us. 'Not enough' has us trying to prove our worth, keep up, compete and scramble our way forward. There is an urgency to the competing mindset as if there is a finish line that we have to rush towards.

So who are you competing with? Your sister, your mom, that community fundraising queen? Who is it exactly? Do you have them in your mind? What is the quality that you see in them that you would like to have more of yourself? This is what it all boils down to. We are striving to be seen to have the same qualities as who ever we are competing with. We may also be trying to prove someone wrong by competing. "See this is the way you do it, watch me. "

You know what I'm going to say about this, it is a waste of energy and effort. There is no one you need to compete with, other than yourself. Compete to be better than you were yesterday and compete with yourself to keep the promises that you say you want to meet.

When you compete with someone you are working with the energy of challenge.

What happens when you push against someone? They push back, right? Now you are both in challenge energy, you spend a whole lot of time here competing and someone 'wins', so what? You are just going to find the next person to challenge and prove yourself right again. This behaviour becomes addictive.

You are unique, no one can actually compete with you and you can't compete with them. Own your unique qualities and find ways to shine your individual light, stop this competing. When you shine your individual light, you encourage others to shine theirs. More light workers please, we need more of this magical energy in the world.

What's possible when you take exquisite care of yourself?

Do you have a sense of what is possible when you take exquisite care of yourself? Have you done it before? What was it like? Can you imagine having all your needs met, being cared for well, doing the work that you love, and feeling emotionally filled up? What would you be doing with your life if this were your reality?

I know there are a lot of questions here. They are valuable questions to be asking. You know those dreams and goals that you have, they are way more likely to come to fruition if you are taking exquisite care of yourself. Otherwise your lack of self care becomes the excuse that you use to not accomplish what you set out to.

I know it gets easy to fall into the distractions, it is not necessary.

Take care of yourself, exquisitely, allow your inhibitions to drop away and make your dreams come true. When you do the work, reach your goals, and feel the success, you create a positive outcome. Your brain will crave the next positive outcome because it feels really good. We need more of the success and positivity surrounding us. It has a profound impact on how we approach all the experiences of our lives.

We say we want success, but we get scared and we allow ourselves to get distracted.

This is where community comes in. Our community of like minded people will help us stay the course and help us ease the fear on our way to accomplishing our goals.

Let yourself dream.

What could be possible if you allowed yourself to take exquisite care of who you are? What if you were accomplishing what you set out to do. Can you feel the energy building, the excitement that is welling up from inside? Allow that to build, it will lead you to where you need to go. It will give you the energy that you need to continue when you would rather stop.

Dream the dreamy dream. What is the worst that could happen? You could fall short of your goal. It will be okay because you are further along on your journey than if you had never started so keep going.

Is it okay to cycle between neglect and luxury?

As far as self care is concerned there are two ends to the spectrum. Luxury and complete neglect. Luxury is the spa adventure, trips away, pampering, pampering, pampering. Neglect - well that doesn't need any further explanation.

We can swing between these two states pretty quickly. Is that okay?

Sure it's okay. There is a time a place for everything. The neglect part is of more concern than swinging towards the luxury unless of course your luxury swing is burning too big a hole in your bank account.

What would be ideal is a moderation and a minor fluctuation between these two states.

The reason I say this is because neglect is a very challenging habit to change because it its reflective of a deep psychological mindset going on. Neglect conjures up the notion that I'm not worth taking care of. We have covered this territory already, and I think it is important to repeat. You are magnificent, whatever shape or size you embody. Taking care of what you have ensures that you will be at your best for the events of your life. Health is something that we often take for granted until we don't have it any longer.

Cycling between neglect and luxury is also evidence that you are not solid in your commitment to self care. Why not? What has you slip in your ability to care for yourself.

What if you aimed for a consistency between luxury and neglect. What would the middle ground be for you?

Chapter 12: How do I keep my forward progress when I don't trust this will last?

Forward progress is not the problem here, your lack of trust is. By being fearful that this will not last you have already decided that it will not. What would it be like for you to believe that you could sustain this?

Oh, oh! There's that compressed process and fear again.

Do you see how this creeps in again. I hate to say it, but you better get used to it. The further you go in creating the life you want to lead, the more this is going to show up. Think of it as a way marker that tells you are on the right track.

You are afraid this will not continue. That could be true, it could stop. It could also be a stepping stone to something better. Released the attachment to any one thing, and let it all unfold. Your fear is having no affect on the reality of your life it is just making you miserable.

If you are afraid of the process coming to an end, that is a bit irrational. What process are you referring to, exactly? You evolving into who you are meant to be? You are still here are you not? You may not have noticed that you are still evolving, the process is continuing, your fear is not necessary.

What's there to trust, you are the common denominator?

There is nothing to trust other than yourself, this is the good news. There is nothing to trust but yourself, this is the bad news. Your life and the quality of it depends on you. It depends on what your are will to commit yourself to. It depends on what you are willing to access, within yourself. It depends on what you are willing to let go of.

Are you willing to let go of the things that are keeping you stuck?

Often we deceive ourselves by saying that we are willing and yet subconsciously we hold on to that thing for dear life. It is safe to hold onto the old way of thinking about ourselves. It's also not very empowering.

When we become willing to trust ourselves, and show it, we get to live our authentic truth. This is new territory, stretching into your potential, there is no rush. Step in, try it on, get used to the idea that you are magnificence. You are free to explore and live into this fact.

There is no progress report, you get to decide.

Who is measuring forward progress anyway? Honestly, no one! Your progress is your progress.

I've never believing in the notion of living outside the box, or taking a big leap.

I feel they are a bit harsh and I avoid this type of talk at all costs because my reaction is always to pull away. Never again will I jump into something that I'm neither ready or able to choose consciously. It's too painful to jump in and then scramble to meet the new needs. The scrambling in uncertainty is what really hurts.

Rather I would like to remain in my intention, decide for myself, choose, and commit to the things that are important to me. Then I create meaningful and lasting change. Then I show up in my world just the way I want to. This is the place of grace and power.

I've waited a long time to arrive at this point in my life. I hope that revealing my journey to you will help you find your way here, quickly, meaningfully, and easily.

Acknowledgments

Robert F. Pope. Honey I could not have created this book without you. Your ongoing love and support have seen this baby through. At times I didn't think I'd finish and you have kept true to the vision that you see for me and this book. Thank you for that vision.

Ryan Van Heck. You are my greatest witness. I adore you. I especially appreciate your steady perspective and cheerleading. "You got this Mom!" has been such a guiding force for me. Thank you darling.

To my coaches along the way. You are amazing people. That is why I have been so drawn to work with you over the years.

Sandi Amorim, your programs, love and ongoing support have been the foundation for me growing into more of myself. Cosmic Creation is the program that put the fire under my butt to create the things important to me. Living a Created Life has given me the courage to look at all the ways I want to craft my delicious life. Thank you, thank you.

Hillary Schneider, your horses and masterful leadership made my gift in the world crystal clear. Without this clear vision I would still be waffling around in the "what if's".

Andrea J. Lee, your Wealthy Thought Leader community was the first place I really felt at home with the peer group of online professionals. Your masterful trainings made it possible for me to see what fierce, generous, kind leadership looked like. I will be forever grateful for your assistance.

Joni Mar, you were my first coach. Guiding me through my coach training and nuances of being a powerful, female leader. Your vision for the world we live in, is remarkable. It is a pleasure to walk with you in this world of coaching.

To my Breakthrough Academy women, you inspire and support me in such a delicious way. I'm truly grateful for all of you.

The Coaches Training Institute. Henry and Karen Kimsey-House, Leslie Lupinsky, Signy Wilson, Jeff Jacobsen, Caroline Hall, Joni Mar, Clive Prout, Mai Vu, Patrick Ryan, Stephanie Lovinger, Ken Mossman, Lauren Power, Lisa Cormier, Rick Tamlyn, Chuck Allen, and the many assistants and participants, I am grateful for this community. Without all of you, I would not have developed into the woman, coach, and author that I am today. Thank you.

References

- James W. Pennebaker, Writing to Heal.
- Jeannette Maw, Pray Rain Journalling.
- Angela Lauria, The Difference.
- Danielle LaPorte, The Fire Starter Sessions.
- Brené Brown, The Gifts of Imperfection.
- Sandy Dow, Thriving in Chaos.
- Mike Dooley, Leveraging the Universe.
- Julia Cameron, The Artist's Way.
- Elizabeth Gilbert, Big Magic.
- Sandi Amorim, The 100 Day Promise.
- Dr. John Matson, Eating Alive.

Clarity Quest: the Program

Purchasing and reading this book is good, but what if you have specific situation in your life that you would like help with?

Here is how you can work directly with Ciel.

http://ellisinstitute.com/programs.html

About the Author

Ciel Ellis, founder and CEO of The Ellis Institute knows what it means to be weighed down by past events. Her story is one of the wounded healer rising above the events of her life that were threatening to consume her brilliant future.

She spent her first 25 years immersed in the details of her life. Which include: being an adopted child, 10 years of sexual abuse and the loss of 11 close friends and family by the age of 22. The deaths included her adoptive father and two of her siblings.

The next 25 years have been spent journeying back to who she really is, re-connecting with her greatness.

Now she is on a mission to reveal the path to freedom so that other women can find their way to this place of empowerment, joy and fulfillment.

For more Information:

www.ellisinstitute.com
ciel@ellisinstitute.com